Monographs in Politics
Editor J W Grove

Administrative Justice

H J ELCOCK

 Longmans

LONGMANS, GREEN AND CO LTD
London and Harlow
*Associated companies, branches and representatives
throughout the world*

SBN 582 48749 8   1001592140

© *Longmans, Green & Co Ltd 1969*
First published 1969

*Printed in Great Britain by
Butler & Tanner Ltd, Frome and London*

EDITOR'S PREFACE

'Justice,' says John Plamenatz, 'has chiefly been used in two senses: giving every man his due, and the setting right of wrong.' If that is so, it is clear that justice is not exclusively a matter for what Dicey called 'the ordinary courts' and we should not expect a sharp differentiation of function between judges and administrators. In the Administrative State especially, we have come to acknowledge the correctness of this view. It is not merely that we expect bureaucrats to act justly (as well as legally) in their dealings with the individual citizen; we now recognise that the administration of justice (in both these senses) is part of the bureaucrat's positive duties. Moreover, law is a body of rules; and it is sometimes unjust to enforce a rule. Equity (which acknowledges that the law is not always just) is not foreign to the English legal system, but the cumbrousness—in large measure the necessary cumbrousness—of legal machinery, and the inflexibility of statute law, on which the Administrative State chiefly rests, and which is binding on the judges, suggest that equity may often be delivered elsewhere than in a court of law. Hence administrative tribunals and public enquiries.

Surprisingly, there has been very little detailed empirical study of these, at least by political scientists interested in public administration, since the publication, forty years ago, of Professor W. A. Robson's path-breaking *Justice and Administrative Law*. The principles have been discussed (some would say discussed *ad nauseam*) by lawyers, long before (and since) the Franks Committee; yet we have remained relatively ignorant of the way they actually work, of the people who serve on them, and of their relationships to the public officials who constitute the regular civil service. Administrative law, as Sir Ivor Jennings taught us, 'is [about] the law relating to the Administration'; Administrative justice is about the due-giving and wrong-righting activities of public officials and their surrogates. Mr Elcock's monograph is a political scientist's contribution to our knowledge of this process.

This series is now nearly three years old and (it is flattering to note) has provoked several competitors. Three or four new titles will be published shortly in the series, and more will follow. The editor continues to aim at original work, chiefly by younger authors, and hopes to maintain his promise to range widely over the field of contemporary political studies.

J. W. GROVE

TABLE OF CONTENTS

PREFACE

'Il n'y a qu'une véritable problème; celle des relations humaines.' These words of the French aviator-author Saint-Exupéry might well serve as a motto for the student of public administration, for the most intriguing and difficult problems of studying any political institution or process arise from the men who operate it. It has been in the frame of mind portrayed by this sentence that I have sought to approach the machinery of administrative justice.

The men and women concerned with this particular sphere of political activity, whether as members of tribunals or their officers, as members and staff of the Council on Tribunals, or as advocates before tribunals and enquiries, solicitors and trade union officials, have been unfailingly helpful and patient, assisting me in attending hearings, and answering a stream of questions which must often have seemed stupid, and occasionally impertinent. To name them would be invidious, but many people went far beyond the call of duty to assist me in my researches: I am deeply grateful to them all.

Apart from those actively involved in administrative justice, there are many other debts of gratitude which I have incurred. Mr Gerald Fowler, Joint Parliamentary Secretary to the Ministry of Technology and M.P. for The Wrekin, was of great assistance in procuring information from government departments and in other ways. The suggestion that there was a need for such a book as this came from my former colleague at Hull, Mr Trevor Smith, who gave me much subsequent advice and encouragement. Professor A. H. Birch read an early draft of my ideas and gave assistance, while Mr N. C. M. Elder read the manuscript and did much to remedy defects of style. Mr C. R. Frost also read the manuscript and filled certain legal deficiencies, and Professor H. W. R. Wade, of Oxford University, did much to remedy my lack of a legal education. I am also indebted to Miss Linda Spall of the Sub-Department of Computation at the University of Hull for her assistance in the preparation of statistical material. Last but by no means least, my friend Mr Robert Baxter, now of the Queen's University of Belfast, has been throughout an apparently bottomless source of ideas, assistance and not least encouragement.

None of these my guides and companions during this task is in any way responsible for such blemishes as remain; for these I am alone responsible.

Hull   HJE

April 1968

ACKNOWLEDGEMENTS

We are indebted to the following for permission to reproduce copyright material:

Ernest Benn Ltd. for extracts from *The New Despotism* by Lord Hewart; The Controller of Her Majesty's Stationery Office for an extract from *The Annual Report of the Council on Tribunals for 1966*; author and The Clarendon Press for an extract from *The Principles of Politics* by J. R. Lucas; the Editor of *New Society* for an extract from an article 'A Better Legal Service: Public Advocates' from issue dated 19th January 1967.

I THE MACHINERY FOR THE REDRESS OF GRIEVANCES IN BRITAIN

It was said once that the British acquired their Empire in a fit of absence of mind; so also have they acquired their system of administrative justice. There was no moment or even period when a system of administrative law was brought into existence: there was no statute or edict which declared the new field of adjudication open. The system just grew piecemeal.

Some administrative tribunals have a long history. The General Commissioners of Income Tax, for example, are the direct descendants of medieval tax collectors, and the areas they cover are still based on the ancient hundreds and wapentakes, and bear no relation to the area of jurisdiction of local tax offices. In the main, though, administrative tribunals are a creation of the present century.

The Englishman's ancient protections against the possibility of arbitrary actions by Government are afforded by three of the main features of our constitution. First, there is his right to parliamentary representation, and of access to his member of parliament, which enables him to have the administration called to account for its misdeeds. Second, the hallowed doctrine of the Separation of Powers assures him of a judiciary independent of the executive which will not hesitate to condemn the latter should it exceed its powers or infringe the rights and liberties of the citizen. Third, the rule of law forbids the Government from acting except in accordance with such enactments and rules of common law as are in force at the time. The guardians of these vital principles of our constitution are Parliament and the courts of law.

However, nowadays many disputes between the citizen and the administration are heard and decided outside these traditional arenas; they are decided by what I have chosen to call the machinery of administrative justice. To call it a system of administrative courts would not only invite misleading comparisons with the French and German administrative courts, but would also imply a uniformity which does not exist in the actual system, which grew up *ad hoc*, and still clearly bears the marks of its piecemeal origin, even after much has been done to tidy the system up. The work of the machinery of administrative justice is at once outside the realm of the courts and linked closely to the administration, and like the courts in that its task is to arbitrate disputes and apply the law of the land to them.

That the machinery of administrative justice is separate from the courts, and not subject to the same obligations as to procedure that are imposed upon the courts of law, was made clear in the famous case of Local Government Board *v.* Arlidge, in 1914,[1] which seems a good point at which to begin an account of the nature of the system and of its development. The case concerned property in the Metropolitan Borough of Hammersmith which the Borough Council had declared to be unfit for human habitation, an order later reaffirmed. This action had involved the holding of two public enquiries under a recent statute, the Local Government Act of 1909, which had transferred the power to confirm these Orders from the County Courts to local authorities, subject to appeal to the Local Government Board, then the central Department charged with the supervision of local authorities. The property owner had appealed against the procedure adopted by the Board, and had won his case in the Court of Appeal, which held that the Board's procedure had not conformed with the rules of 'natural justice' and that their decision was therefore invalid. The Board then appealed to the House of Lords which reversed the decision, Lord Haldane delivering a judgment which laid down that law and administration were separate fields, and that the standards applicable to the first were not applicable to the second. Lord Haldane said:

> It is obvious that the Act of 1909 introduced a change of policy. The jurisdiction, both as regards original applications and as regards appeals, was in England transferred from Courts of justice to the local authority and the Local Government Board, both of them administrative bodies, and it is necessary to consider what consequences this change of policy imported. . . . The result of [the public] enquiry must . . . be taken, in the absence of directions to the contrary,[2] to be intended to be reached by [the Department's] ordinary procedure.

[1] A.C. (H.L.) 1915, at 120.   [2] i.e. in the statue.

Thus in cases where adjudication was made the responsibility of Government Departments rather than the courts, the demands of 'natural justice' do not apply, and the remedies available in the event of irregular procedure in court are not available to the same degree.[1] Administrative procedures may not be judged by judicial standards. The High Court still has the ancient powers of prohibition, *mandamus* and *certiorari* where the requirements of the law have not been complied with, but the Arlidge decision made it more difficult to attack tribunal or enquiry procedure in the courts.

During the present century, the machinery of administrative justice has proliferated steadily; it has been a corollary of the extension of state activity. As social security schemes were introduced from 1911 onwards they brought with them a need for some method of deciding borderline or dubious claims to benefits where the application of statutes or regulations was unclear, and the usual response was the creation of an administrative tribunal. These bodies were often closely linked to the department they served; their members were usually appointed by the Minister, who also provided their staff and accommodation. However scrupulous a department might be in not seeking unduly to control or influence tribunals, the temptation was always there, and public suspicions were inevitably aroused. Justice might often be done, but it was certainly not seen to be done.

Towards the end of the nineteen-twenties, concern over the multiplying number of tribunals outside the courts began to mount. As social benefit schemes were introduced, especially under the first Labour Government in 1924, the machinery of administrative justice had been expanded and to some persons it appeared to be a part of the Socialist juggernaut which threatened, as they believed, to extinguish Liberty under a blanket of regulation and control. At any rate, the problem was big enough by 1928 to arouse public concern, and in that year the first of two books commenting on the system and urging reforms was published. This was Professor William Robson's *Justice and Administrative Law*,[2] in which he expressed concern at the way the system was working and promulgated nineteen principles which he

[1] Lord Haldane said earlier in the judgment in Arlidge's case that 'where the duty of deciding an appeal is imposed, those whose duty it is to decide must act judicially', but administrative bodies are masters of their own procedures to a greater degree than the courts.

[2] Macmillan, 1928; reprinted 1947.

deemed essential if it were to inspire public confidence and if the citizen appearing before tribunals or enquiries were to be sure of fair treatment. These principles included consistency of decisions, and independence from Departments, to be ensured by the creation of 'definite tribunals consisting of public servants specially nominated for the purpose by the responsible Minister', who should not perform any of 'the ordinary duties of the Department' apart from their duties as tribunal members. Tribunals should be given power to compel production of documents and witnesses, should give reasoned decisions and above all, should not be subject to covert control by Ministers or civil servants; to this end Professor Robson demanded that in future, 'the control exercised by the Minister over the work of the tribunal should . . . be exclusively confined to instructions contained in public documents'. Furthermore, the persons who heard the evidence ought to decide the case, an attack on the enquiry procedure, where an inspector hears the evidence but the Minister decides the case.[1] These principles amounted to a demand for independence and fair procedure commensurate with those obtaining in the courts of law.

The following year there appeared another book making many of the same points as had Professor Robson, but couched in more dramatic terms. This was the then Lord Chief Justice's attack on the growth of administrative powers, *The New Despotism*.[2] It is full of dire warnings of the consequences of current developments; early in the book Lord Hewart warned that

> Much toil, and not a little blood, have been spent in bringing slowly into being a polity wherein the people make their laws, and independent judges administer them. If that edifice is to be overthrown, let the overthrow be accomplished openly. Never let it be said that liberty and justice, having with difficulty been won, were suffered to be abstracted or impaired in a fit of absence of mind.[3]

Much of the book is taken up with a denunciation of the growing volume of delegated legislation, but Lord Hewart had some harsh words also for the machinery of administrative justice. He described the continental administrative courts, where 'the rights and obligations

[1] Robson, *op. cit.*, p. 315 f.
[2] Lord Hewart, L. C. J., *The New Despotism* (Benn, 1929).
[3] Hewart, *op. cit.*, pp. 16–17.

of all servants of the State, and also of all private individuals in relation to servants of the State acting in their official capacity, as well as the procedure for enforcing those rights and obligations, are governed by special rules which are, in general, administered by special tribunals' and goes on to contrast with these continental systems, which he greatly admired, the British system, which he denounced as 'administrative lawlessness', saying that

> It is not, but it ought to be, common knowledge that there is in this country a considerable number of statutes, most of them passed during the last twenty years, which have vested in public officials, to the exclusion of the jurisdiction of the Courts of Law, the power of deciding questions of a judicial nature. . . . To apply the terms administrative 'law' and administrative 'justice' to such a system, or negation of system, is really grotesque. The exercise of arbitrary power is neither law nor justice, administrative or at all. The very conception of 'law' is a conception of something involving the application of known rules and principles, and a regular course of procedure. There are no rules or principles which can be said to be the rules or principles of this astonishing variety of administrative 'law', nor is there any regular course of procedure for its application. It is possible, no doubt, that the public official who decides questions in pursuance of the powers given to his department does act, or persuades himself that he acts, on some general rules or principles. But if so, they are entirely unknown to anybody outside the department, and of what value is a so-called 'law' of which nobody has any knowledge?[1]

To Lord Hewart, the system seemed neither legal nor just; it was simply unfettered discretion given to officials. He admitted that the system was cheap, but if bought at the cost of sacrificing justice, it was too dearly bought, and he concluded that this was merely an excuse put forward to disguise the true purpose of the system; '*Sunt lacrimae rerum*—also *crocodilorum*. Things have their tears, and crocodiles have theirs.'[2] This bitter, emotive attack further aroused parliamentary and public concern to a point at which the Government felt constrained to have the system of administrative justice investigated, and to this end appointed an official committee under Lord Donoughmore. The

[1] Hewart, *op. cit.*, pp. 37–8.   [2] Hewart, *op. cit.*, p. 76.

B

Donoughmore Committee sat for three years and produced a report[1] in which, after an extended analysis of the term 'quasi-judicial', which appeared in their terms of reference, they recommended that all administrative tribunals should in future be obliged to conform to the principles of 'natural justice', which they enumerated as follows:

1. No man should be judge in his own cause. The Committee commented that 'Bias from strong and sincere conviction as to public policy may operate as a more serious disqualification than pecuniary interest.'
2. No party should be condemned unheard, and parties should be informed in good time of the case they would have to meet at the hearing.
3. Reasoned decisions should be given by the tribunal.
4. Inspectors' reports after public enquiries should be published.[2]

These were their most important recommendations; they would ensure open, impartial proceedings. The Committee refused to recommend the creation of a unified system of administrative courts on the French pattern, though urged to do so in evidence submitted by Professor Robson.[3] The creation of such a system, they said, would be 'inconsistent with the sovereignty of Parliament and the supremacy of the law'.[4] The pillars of the constitution must not be weakened, come what may.

In any event, the Committee's recommendations were mainly ignored. In 1932 there were more pressing matters for Governments to think about. More was to be heard of these issues in later years, for the machinery of administrative justice continued to grow, unchecked and largely unsupervised. The Unemployment Assistance Act of 1934 brought new tribunals into existence to hear disputes over refusals of benefit, rates of grant and conditions attached to grants. In April 1939, as war loomed near, Mr Chamberlain announced the first arrangements for conscription into the armed forces, including the creation of tribunals to hear claims for exemption on the ground that the subject

---

[1] *Report of the Committee on Ministers' Powers*, Cmd 4060, H.M.S.O., 1932 (hereafter referred to by command number).

[2] Cmd 4060, para. 19.

[3] But he did not despair, and urged the same course on the Franks Committee more than twenty years later.

[4] Cmd 4060, para. 19.

had a conscientious objection to military service. As the war went on, more and more regulations governing the movement of labour were necessary, and often tribunals were created to apply them, considering such matters as whether workmen should be allowed to leave factories engaged on work of strategic importance, and whether conscription should be deferred on grounds of hardship.[1] Still there was no common standard for tribunals. Each Department, and often each tribunal, operated in the way it thought best.[2] Where there was a further appeal to a superior body, some element of consistency was possible; otherwise it was every tribunal for itself. Under the stress of war, the problems to which this gave rise were ignored; everyone coped as best they could.

The Courts also had a part in preventing the system developing the judicial virtue of consistency by restricting severely the extent to which tribunals and officials deciding enquiry cases could openly follow precedent. In contrast to the position in the United States, the British Courts have laid down that administrators taking decisions may not follow precedent; each case must be decided on its own merits. The first case, in 1918, that of The King *v.* London County Council, *ex parte* Corrie[3] concerned a volunteer worker for the blind who applied for permission to sell a pamphlet, *The British Blind,* in a council-owned park, a request which was refused on the ground that previously the council had passed a general resolution that in future permission to sell articles in parks under their control would be refused; they would not exercise the discretion to permit such sale given them under a bye-law. The case was appealed, and the council's decision was invalidated on the ground that an administrative authority must exercise a discretion where it has been given one, in every case coming before it. Mr Justice Darling, delivering judgment, referred to a series of nineteenth-century cases in which a similar rule had been laid down for licensing magistrates, and went on:

> This rule must be made absolute. The Court can come to no other decision without infringing the principles governing the hearing of

[1] See R. S. W. Pollard, ed. *Administrative Tribunals at Work* (Stevens, 1950), chapters 1 and 2, for a description of these tribunals.
[2] D. Hayes, *The Challenge of Conscience* (Allen & Unwin, 1949) shows this clearly in the case of conscientious objector tribunals, in chapters 3 and 4.
[3] (1918) 1 *K.B.* at 68.

applications for licences to sell intoxicating liquors. It has been laid down that the body on whom is conferred the jurisdiction of granting such licences must hear each application on its merits and cannot come to a general resolution to refuse a licence to everybody who does not conform to some particular requirement. . . . In my view, this case . . . is within the principle of the licensing cases, and the applicant has a right to move the Court in this form.

Thus a rule made in the nineteenth century for licensing justices was extended to cover administrative authorities in general, creating a situation totally unlike that in America, where administrative authorities have been bound by the courts to follow their own precedents, to the extent that the National Labour Relations Board was forbidden to depart from its own ruling that back pay should be awarded to dismissed employees only from the date when their complaint was filed.[1] In America, bodies carrying out functions similar to our administrative tribunals are obliged to follow their own precedents, and this obligation has been imposed for the very reason that Lord Hewart was so affrighted by the way the British system was developing. Administrative lawlessness was to be avoided; in the words of Mr Justice Frankfurter, delivering judgment in the Supreme Court in the case of Vitarelli *v.* Seaton:

An executive agency must be rigorously held to the standards by which it professes its actions to be judged. Accordingly, if dismissal from employment is based on a defined procedure, even if generous beyond the requirements that bind the agency, that procedure must be scrupulously observed. This judicial rule of administrative law is now firmly established and, if I may add, *rightly so*. He that takes the procedural sword shall perish with that sword.[2]

In America administrators must be consistent; in Britain they may not ensure that they are so by following precedents or general rules, as the Corrie case made clear. However, in The King *v.* Port of London

[1] National Labour Relations Board *v.* Malt Tool Co. 119 F. 2d 700 (7th Cir. 1941), cited in H. W. R. Wade, 'Anglo-American Administrative Law: Some Reflections' in *Law Quarterly Review*, vol. 81 (1965), 374. I am indebted to Professor Wade's article for drawing my attention to the contrast between British and American practice.
[2] 359 *U.S.*535 (1959) cited in Wade, *op. cit.*, at 376. My italics.

Authority, *ex parte* Kynoch Ltd,[1] the doctrine was somewhat qualified; an administrative body could, 'in the honest exercise of its discretion', adopt a policy, and could, 'without refusing to hear an applicant, intimate to him what that policy is, and that after hearing him it will in accordance with its policy decide against him, unless there is something exceptional in his case'.[2] The authority can formulate a policy, but must hear each case and judge it on the merits, and consider whether in this case the policy should be applied or not. If this is not done, the decision is liable to be quashed by the Courts under the Corrie rule.

In later years, the doctrine was applied to adjudicatory bodies, including administrative tribunals. The first such case was that of The King *v.* Paddington and Marylebone Rent Tribunal,[3] in which a local authority had referred a large number of tenancies in a certain apartment block to the rent tribunal after two tenants had been granted reductions in rent by the tribunal. The local authority relied on these successes to guarantee success in the remaining cases; a position which the tribunal accepted, an action condemned in the High Court when the landlord appealed; Lord Goddard denounced the procedure adopted at the tribunal hearing by the local authority when he said in delivering judgment:

> The proceedings at the hearing were truly remarkable. The Council called no evidence; they did not put forward a single argument. Their representative merely informed the tribunal that as there had been two previous references by tenants, the Council had referred the remainder of the contracts of tenancy to the tribunal. . . . We cannot agree that, in the circumstances of this case, the mere fact that two tenants had of their own motion complained and obtained some relief is any justification for this wholesale reference by the Council.

Each case must be considered on its own merits. This had been the ruling in *Corrie's* case and it was now applied to tribunals. In 1962 this happened again, this time relating to the Transport Tribunal, in the case of Merchandise Transport Ltd. *v.* British Transport Commission and Others[4] when the judges of the Court of Appeal showed themselves firm defenders of the Corrie rule. Lord Justice Sellars said that

---

[1] (1919) 1 *K.B.* at 176. [2] *Ibid.*, at 184. [3] (1949) 1 *K.B.* 666.
[4] (1962) 2 *Q.B.* at 173.

'where discretion lies it should not be hidebound by authority' and Lord Justice Devlin in a concurring judgment said that while 'a series of reasoned judgments such as the [Transport] tribunal gives is bound to disclose the general principles upon which it proceeds', a feature 'not only inevitable, but desirable' since it enabled the industry under the tribunal's supervision to know, 'in a general way' how applications were likely to be treated, nonetheless this could not permit the tribunal to 'make rules which prevent or excuse either itself or the licensing authorities from examining each case on its merits. . . . A tribunal must not pursue consistency at the expense of the merits of individual cases.' This, then, is the legal rule in Britain governing administrative decisions, whether taken by local authorities, government departments, administrative tribunals or licensing justices. The extent to which administrators may follow precedent is very restricted.

The system is thus basically inchoate, if one may use this word without prejudice to the issue. There can be no binding precedent for decisions; equally, procedure is left to the individual tribunal to a large extent. It is an *ad hoc* system meting out what often looks very like justice at the gate; for this reason it has from time to time come under suspicion. This had happened in the late nineteen-twenties; after the Second World War two more battles were to be fought before administrative justice was given a major overhaul.

The first battle concerned public enquiries, which were to become a major bone of contention in the years between 1947 and 1958. After the war, it was proposed to build a New Town to accommodate persons moved out from the slum areas of London, and the site chosen was at Stevenage, in Hertfordshire. A public enquiry was held in accordance with the procedure required by the New Towns Act of 1946, but after the Minister's decision had been announced a group of local residents who had been objectors at the enquiry appealed to the High Court for an Order to remove the decision to the High Court, where it might be quashed, on the grounds that the Minister had not acted within the powers conferred upon him by the Act and had not complied with its requirements, and also that the Minister had revealed in a speech made in 1946 that he had decided to have the New Town sited at Stevenage and could not therefore have given fair and proper consideration to the objectors. It was an expression of discontent with the enquiry procedure, whereby objectors address a person with no power to decide, whose report then disappeared in the 'caverns measureless to man' of Whitehall to be pronounced upon by a Minister who had never heard the objectors put their cases forward. The case eventually reached the House of Lords, where the Minister's decision was upheld on a ground which confirmed the independence of administrative procedures from the restraints of judicial procedure; Lord Thankerton said in judgment that under the terms of the New Towns Act:

> In my opinion, no judicial, or quasi-judicial, duty was imposed on the respondent,[1] and any reference to judicial duty or bias is irrelevant in the present case. The respondent's duties . . . are, in my opinion, purely administrative, but the Act prescribes certain methods of, or steps in, discharge of that duty.[2]

This meant that a statutory enquiry was simply a prescribed stage in the process of reaching a decision. As Lord Thankerton said, the enquiry's object was only to 'inform the mind of the Minister', and was not in any way a judicial procedure. It could not, therefore, be attacked in the Courts on the ground that it did not measure up to judicial standards of fairness or impartiality. The judgment in the Arlidge case over thirty years before, was given further confirmation in the Stevenage case.

A few years later a new storm broke, not directly over tribunals and enquiries, but which was ultimately to result in major reforms, intended to give more assurance that justice was done, and that the citizen's rights and property were properly protected from the mistakes or abuses of administrators. The occasion for these reforms was the so-called 'Crichel Down Affair', in 1954. It is not necessary to go into any detail in describing this imbroglio, as the facts are well known and the case is something of a *cause célèbre*; it will suffice to say that civil servants in the Ministry of Agriculture attempted to avoid dealing with a member of a landowning family, one Commander Marten, who appeared to them to be an awkward customer, by covertly denying him the opportunity to bid for an area of Crown land to be offered for sale to the public. Commander Marten brought their action to the attention of his member of parliament and began a storm which culminated in

[1] i.e. the Minister.
[2] Franklin and Others *v*. Minister of Town and Country Planning, *H.L.* (1948) *A.C.*87.

the resignation of the Minister of Agriculture, Sir Thomas Dugdale.[1] Apart from bringing the political career of the unfortunate Dugdale to an abrupt end, the affair aroused considerable concern over the procedure for the compulsory acquisition of land, for which reason the Government decided, with doubtful logic, to appoint a committee to investigate the entire field of tribunals and enquiries. This Committee sat under the chairmanship of Sir Oliver Franks,[2] and was given the following terms of reference:

> To consider and make recommendations on:
> (*a*) The constitution and working of tribunals other than the ordinary courts of law, constituted under any Act of Parliament by a Minister of the Crown or for the purposes of a Minister's functions.
> (*b*) The working of such administrative procedures as include the holding of an enquiry or hearing by or on behalf of a Minister on an appeal or as the result of objections or representations, and in particular the procedure for the compulsory purchase of land.[3]

As a response to the Crichel Down case, the terms of reference were very wide indeed; only the last clause of the second paragraph could be said to bear any relevance to the subject of the furore. The Committee reported in 1957, after an extensive investigation of the machinery of administrative justice, and the taking of a good deal of evidence, some of which advocated the introduction of a system of administrative courts on the French model, as proposed by Professor Robson to the Donoughmore Committee before the war.

Detailed examination of the Committee's Report may be left until later; we shall frequently have cause to refer to their findings and recommendations in the course of this account. Here it will suffice to note that the Committee made ninety-five recommendations, chief

---

[1] There are several accounts of this affair; the reader might consult G. Marshall and G. C. Moodie, *Some Problems of the Constitution* (Hutchinson, 1964), Lord Morrison, *Government and Parliament* (O.U.P., 1962). Articles in *Public Administration* by D. N. Chester (1954) and S. E. Finer (1956) will throw some extra light on the affair, if more is needed.

[2] Now the Baron Franks of Headington.

[3] *Report of the Committee on Administrative Tribunals and Enquiries*, Cmnd 218 (H.M.S.O., 1957), hereafter referred to by command number, terms of reference on p. iii.

among which was that two councils, one for England and Wales and a second for Scotland, should be established to undertake the task of scrutinising continuously the working of the machinery of administrative justice.[1] They rejected the proposals for administrative courts, like the Donoughmore Committee before them; this was their substitute, designed to ensure more consistency, at least in procedure and practice. The Committee's second main contribution was the promulgation of standards by which the working of tribunals and enquiries should be judged; they summarised these as 'openness, fairness and impartiality', which criteria formed the basis for all their recommendations.

The Donoughmore Report had been ignored; not so its successor, the Franks Report. It was presented to Parliament in July 1957; the following year two major steps were taken towards its implementation by the Government. First, the Ministry of Housing and Local Government issued a circular to local authorities enjoining them to ensure that their actions at public enquiries conformed as nearly as possible to the standards set out in the Franks Report, and announcing a number of changes in the Ministry's own procedure. It urged local authorities to be more careful than they had previously been to explain their reasons when notifying members of the public of decisions displeasing to them, such as refusals of planning permission. The local authorities were already obliged to furnish reasons for such refusals, and the Ministry now urged a more faithful execution of this duty:

> It is important that [the] statement [of reasons] should be full enough to give the applicant adequate understanding of the reasons for the authority's decision. For example, it is not ordinarily sufficient to say merely that the development 'would be injurious to amenity' or would 'be contrary to the provisions of the Development plan'. In the former case, it should be explained what is the amenity that would be injured; in the latter precisely what provisions in the Plan are involved and how they apply.[2]

In the next paragraph, the authority is advised to notify the applicant of any Government policy, directive or circular they have taken into account. In short, the applicant should know in full the case against him, which he will have to meet if he appeals to the Minister; he may

---

[1] *Ibid.*, para. 43, chapter 11, and Recommendations 29 to 33.
[2] Ministry of Housing and Local Government Circular 9/58, para. 7.

accept the arguments against him and decide not to appeal; in any case, he has a chance to answer the authority's case with his own. Later the circular proclaimed that a new code of procedure for enquiries would be issued by the Ministry, and that Ministry witnesses from Transport, Housing, and any other department which 'has expressed positive views for or against a proposal' would present themselves for examination at the enquiry. Finally, the circular promised the publication of inspectors' reports and a letter from the Minister to the parties setting out his decision and reasons.[1] This seemed to herald a considerable improvement in enquiry procedure, especially in the matter of informing parties of the official case they would have to meet, and as regards the openness of decisions.

The second governmental action to implement the Committee's recommendations was of a more general nature. The Tribunals and Enquiries Act of 1958 provided for the creation of a Council on Tribunals of 10 to 15 members, with a Scottish Committee in addition, charged:

(a) To keep under review the constitution and working of . . . tribunals . . . and, from time to time, to report on their constitution and working.

(b) To consider and report on such matters as may be referred to the Council under this Act with respect to tribunals other than the ordinary Courts of Law. . . .[2]

(c) To consider and report on such matters as may be referred . . . to the Council or as the Council may determine to be of special importance, with respect to administrative procedures involving, or which may involve, the holding by or on behalf of a Minister of a statutory enquiry, or any such procedure.[3]

The Council was thus given a continuing supervision of tribunals under its jurisdiction, and a power to investigate obligatory enquiries, though not those held at a Minister's discretion, which might be brought to its notice. The Act nowhere defines a tribunal; the bodies which are to come under the Council's supervision are simply listed

---

[1] Ministry of Housing and Local Government Circular 9/58, paras 8–26.

[2] Thus the Act elsewhere provides that new regulations relating to tribunals shall be submitted to the Council for their opinion.

[3] Tribunals and Enquiries Act, 6 & 7 Eliz. 2, ch. 16, Section 1, para. 1.

in the First Schedule to the Act, to which others may be added by statutory instrument. The Council is obliged to report annually to the Lord Chancellor and the Secretary of State for Scotland and can also issue special reports as it sees fit.

The Tribunals and Enquiries Act also empowers the Lord Chancellor to appoint persons to panels from which tribunal chairmen are chosen by the appropriate Department or other authority,[1] and from the Act's coming into force, members of most tribunals were removable only with the Lord Chancellor's consent. Section 8, paragraph 1 prescribes that:

> No power of a Minister or of the Lord President of the Court of Session to make, approve, confirm, or concur in procedural rules for any such tribunal as is specified in the First Schedule to this Act shall be exerciseable except after consultation with the Council.

This gives the Council a right to be consulted on all new procedural rules, and thus the Act provided for ensuring that all such rules would conform to the standards of 'openness, fairness and impartiality' laid down by the Franks Committee.

In Section 12, paragraph 1, the Act commands that tribunals and Ministers giving decisions after the holding of a public enquiry give the reasons for their decisions, in writing if requested to do so, unless there are considerations of security, or if to do so would not be in the interests of 'persons primarily concerned'. As we shall see later, this provision has been enforced with considerable vigour by the courts.[2] The Act also provides for appeal from tribunals on points of law to the High Court in certain cases.[3]

Shortly after the passage of the Act, the Council on Tribunals began its work. Since then, it has issued nine annual Reports and a number of special Reports.[4] The Council's work features often in what follows, but for an excellent account of it I would refer the reader to an article by Professor J. F. Garner which appeared in *Public Law*, 1965. Quite a lot of the Council's time has been occupied by the consideration of

---

[1] *Ibid.*, Section 3, para. 1.

[2] See chapter 5. The cases are: *Ex Parte* Woodhouse, *The Times* Law Report, 18 June 1960; *In Re* Poyser Mills Arbitration, (1964) 2 *Q.B.* 467, and Givaudan and Co., Ltd *v.* Minister of Housing and Local Government, (1967) I *W.L.R.* 250.

[3] Section 9, para. 1.

[4] Published as appendices to the annual Reports.

new regulations relating to tribunals; on average, about a dozen sets of new procedural rules are scrutinized every year. Professor Garner formed a high opinion of the Council's work in this respect; he says that 'many files in the Council's office . . . bear testimony to the extent of consultation that has taken place',[1] and he gives a number of examples of this process at work. A particularly important one was the consultation with the Ministry of Housing in 1962, on the new procedural rules for public enquiries drawn up by the Ministry in fulfilment of the promise made four years before.[2] The Council also investigates complaints from individuals about tribunals and enquiries, an activity which takes up a little over one-third of the time of the Council's office staff, though many complaints do not reach the Council itself. Many are trivial or irrelevant, but some have resulted in the Council's most widely reported actions, such as their investigation of the 'Chalkpit case' in 1961.[3] The Council regards complaints from the public as an important piece of assistance in their work; in their first Report they said 'We are commonly described as "watchdogs" for the public, and we must look to them in large measure to inform us of matters requiring to be watched.'[4]

Another part of the Council's duties is to visit tribunals, a duty carried out by its members individually. They have had some difficulty in gaining entrance to some tribunals held *in camera*, and especially in securing permission to retire with the tribunal and observe their deliberations.[5] Many of these difficulties have now been resolved, although in some cases this has required some diligent quarrying on the part of the Council; it took them five years to obtain entrance to hearings of Service Committees and the National Health Service Tribunal[6] and it was only in 1965 that the Minister of Pensions and National Insurance agreed to alter the regulations relating to National Insurance Local Tribunals in order to permit members of the Council on Tribunals to retire with the members of the tribunals at the Chairman's discretion, although the refusal of successive Ministers to do this earlier had given rise to adverse comment in several previous

---

[1] Garner, *op. cit.*, p. 327.
[2] *Ibid.*, pp. 333–4, and the Report of the Council on Tribunals for 1962.
[3] Fourth Report (H.M.S.O., 1963), part III.
[4] *First Report of the Council on Tribunals* (H.M.S.O., 1960), para. 128.
[5] See Garner *op. cit.*, pp. 338–9, and the annual Reports of the Council.
[6] Sixth Report (H.M.S.O., 1965), para. 21.

Reports of the Council.[1] Since its creation, the Council on Tribunals has covered a considerable area and has certainly led to an improvement in tribunal procedure, besides performing certain functions akin to those of the Scandinavian Ombudsman. The Council has no powers: it is purely an advisory body, but in the field of administrative justice it is a power for good. In 1966 a new Act extended its powers to cover enquiries held at ministerial discretion.[2]

The Franks Report also foreshadowed perhaps the most widely publicised development in the field of the redress of grievances in recent years, the ultimately successful agitation for the appointment of a British Ombudsman. The Franks Committee pointed out that

> over most of the field of public administration no formal procedure is provided for objecting or deciding on objections. For example, when foreign currency or a scarce commodity such as petrol or coal is rationed or allocated, there is no other body to which an individual applicant can appeal if the responsible administrative authority decides to allow him less than he has requested. Of course, the aggrieved individual can always complain to the appropriate administrative authority, to his Member of Parliament, to a representative organisation, or to the Press. But there is no formal procedure on which he can insist.[3]

Some people thought there should be such a procedure, which could provide for an investigation on behalf of the citizen and seek redress if his complaint proved to be justified. In 1961 this comment by the Franks Committee was followed by a report of a committee of 'Justice', the British section of the International Commission of Jurists, under the chairmanship of Sir John Whyatt, whose chief proposal was the institution of an Ombudsman, or 'Parliamentary Commissioner' for Britain to investigate complaints of maladministration. The Whyatt Committee also urged extension of the system of administrative tribunals.[4] The Council on Tribunals for their part welcomed the

---

[1] Seventh Report (H.M.S.O., 1966), para. 6. For previous comment see especially the Fourth Report (H.M.S.O., 1963), para. 21, and the Fifth and Sixth Reports (for 1963 and 1964).

[2] Tribunals and Enquiries Act 1966. Eliz. 2 (1966), ch. 43.

[3] Cmnd 218, para. 10.

[4] Lord Shawcross, ed., *The Citizen and the Administration: the redress of grievances* (Stevens, 1961). See Marshall and Moodie, *op. cit.*, and D. C. Rowat, ed., *The*

proposals in their Fourth Report, though seeming a little fearful lest
they might be ignored by the public if an Ombudsman were appointed,
they sought and obtained a promise from the then Lord Chancellor
that they would be consulted before any action was taken.[1] In any case,
the proposal proved too radical for the Government to stomach, and
on 8 November 1962 the Attorney-General[2] made a statement in the
House of Commons rejecting the Whyatt proposals because they were
'incompatible with the principle of Ministerial responsibility to Parliament', because 'any substantial extension of the system of reference to
tribunals would lead to inflexibility and delay in administration, and
that the appointment of a Parliamentary Commissioner would seriously
interfere with the prompt and efficient dispatch of public business'.
Finally, the Attorney-General made the self-satisfied statement that
the existing safeguard against maladministration afforded to the
citizen by his right of access to his Member of Parliament was still
'adequate'.[3] The Labour Party did not share this view and in *The New
Britain*, their manifesto for the 1964 General Election, gave a promise
to institute a Parliamentary Commissioner, if elected, a promise which
they redeemed first by the issue of a White Paper in 1965;[4] this was
followed by a Bill, which though lost once through the calling of a
second General Election in March 1966, was finally passed, though
somewhat diluted, in 1967.[5] At the time of writing, the first British
Ombudsman, Sir Edmund Compton, is settling into his new job, and
has issued his first report, condemning the action of the Ministry of
Social Security in failing to pay a war disability pension. He is debarred
from investigating matters where the citizen is entitled to a hearing
before a tribunal,[6] and he is *ex officio* a member of the Council on
Tribunals.[7] Some degree of liaison with the Council is thus ensured,

---

Ombudsman, Citizen's Defender (Allen & Unwin, 1965), chapter 10 (by Geoffrey
Marshall) for excellent accounts of the Whyatt proposals and of later developments.
For arguments for and against the proposal see Rowat, *op. cit.*, chapter 17 (Louis
Blom-Cooper and J. D. B. Mitchell).

[1] Fourth Report (H.M.S.O., 1963), para. 17.
[2] The late Sir John Hobson, Q.C.
[3] 666 *H. of C. Debates* 5s, cols. 1125–6.
[4] *The Parliamentary Commissioner for Administration*, Cmnd 2767, H.M.S.O.,
1965.
[5] Eliz. 2 (1967), ch. 13.
[6] The Parliamentary Commissioner Act, Section 5, para. 2(a).
[7] *Ibid.*, Section 1, para. 5.

and already the Parliamentary Commissioner has passed complaints within the Council's sphere to them. But his relations with the Council and with the whole system of tribunals and enquiries have not been worked out in any detail, and he is another addition to what remains an essentially *ad hoc* system, although since the 1958 Act the Council on Tribunals and the Courts have brought about the end of a good deal of slackness and have given greater uniformity to the system. It remains to be seen how the relations between the Ombudsman and the tribunal system will finally develop. In what follows, we shall see that despite the reforms of the last nine years the system still bears clearly the marks of its diverse origins.

II THE LIFE AND WORK OF TRIBUNALS AND ENQUIRIES

The importance of tribunals and enquiries as a part of the machinery of justice has sometimes been held in doubt. Some would say that they do not really merit the concern either of prestigious committees or of academics and jurists. At the time of the establishment of the Council on Tribunals, Professor J. A. G. Griffith suggested that it was a body too distinguished in membership to be asked to bother itself with tribunals and enquiries. The Council, he said,

> is a team of solid merit, considerable experience, outstanding ability in two or three of its members. . . . It is certainly capable of winning the Battle of Blenheim.[1] But its actual job will be rather different. The principal function of the Council will be to look at the procedure of tribunals and to report how they can be improved. That is certainly a fairly sizeable nut. But it needs a small and rather special sort of cracker. Not a steamroller.[2]

Tribunals and enquiries are not worthy of the concern of eminent men, says Professor Griffith, since, in his view, no great issue of justice is involved. The establishment of tribunals has been a matter of convenience; 'the usual reasons for their establishment are well known to be their cheapness, their informality, their expertness and the speed with which decisions can be obtained'.[3] In short, their relationship to the courts of law, in Professor Griffith's view, is somewhat akin to that of snoek to salmon. Other writers have declared, often passionately, that the basic rights and privileges of the citizen are at stake; Lord Hewart's book, *The New Despotism*, argued that administrative judicial procedures are often 'a travesty of justice'[4] and sometimes 'pure despotism'.[5] Such emotive statements could come only from one who

[1] Professor Griffith was alluding to the struggle to improve tribunal procedure and to introduce supervision over them which culminated in the Franks Report and the Tribunals and Enquiries Act of 1958. See p. 24.

[2] J. A. G. Griffith, 'Tribunals and Enquiries', in *Modern Law Review*, vol. 22 (1959), 125 f, quotation p. 131.

[3] *Ibid.*, p. 129.   [4] Hewart, *op. cit.*, p. 47.   [5] Hewart, *op. cit.*, p. 50.

believed that the need to scrutinise the working of tribunals and enquiries was a matter of importance. In the present chapter we shall see that in terms of the sheer volume of work they do, and its variety, tribunals and enquiries do nowadays play a very significant role in the relationship in Britain between authority and the individual.

The average person, even the student, can get but little impression of this role. The figures of tribunal work are not available in any readily accessible form; where they are available at all they are tucked away in official reports, frequently in appendices, and often they are not generally available at all. As far as the nature of their work is concerned, no work has been published on tribunals since that of Mr Robert Pollard and colleagues in 1950.[1] The wide range of the problems covered is also to some degree concealed by the customary division between tribunals and enquiries; a division unfortunately retained by the Franks Committee, who assert that 'all, or nearly all, tribunals apply rules. No ministerial decision of the kind denoted by the second part of our terms of reference is reached in this way.'[2] Hence one might think that the work of tribunals and that of enquiries was of a clearly defined kind in each case. As we shall see later, this is not so, and many of the problems we shall discuss in what follows relate as much to enquiries as they do to tribunals and vice versa. To divide the field down the middle like this is an oversimplification which can lead the student of administrative justice astray.

First let us deal with the purely quantitative question of the work load of tribunals and enquiries. That they are, to say the least, ubiquitous dispensers of justice was recognised by the Franks Committee. They pointed out that but for the emergence of tribunals and enquiries, the courts would by now have been swamped by the volume of litigation which the expansion of Government activity in the present century would have brought in its train. As Government activity expands, so the points of possible contention between itself and its subjects, or between subject and subject, have expanded too, and if all the new areas of dispute had been made the responsibility of the courts, these would now, in the opinion of the Franks Committee, be 'grossly overburdened', and the necessary expansion would certainly have resulted in a dilution harmful to the quality of our judges.[3]

[1] R. S. W. Pollard, ed. *Administrative Tribunals at Work* (Stevens, 1950).
[2] Cmnd 218, para. 31.   [3] Cmnd 218, para. 39.

c

The Franks Committee gave a few figures which indicated the size of the part played by tribunals and enquiries in our present day administration. They found that in 'some recent years', before 1957, rent tribunals had dealt with 15,000 cases, National Insurance tribunals with 50 to 60,000, and the Ministry of Housing had heard some 6,000 planning appeals each year.[1] In the first part of this chapter we can expand on this and obtain a picture of the volume of work done both from the standpoint of the individual tribunal and from a national viewpoint.

The case load and area covered by any one tribunal varies widely between different types of tribunal. In recent years there have been some amalgamations, and a tendency to allot new functions to existing tribunals rather than create new ones, and also to enlarge the areas covered by a single body, a tendency in accordance with the Franks Committee's recommendations that 'Whenever it is proposed to establish a new tribunal consideration should first be given to the possibility of vesting the jurisdiction in an existing tribunal',[2] and that where possible they should be amalgamated.[3] In the case of rent tribunals, from 78 in 1948, their number was reduced to 41 by 1960.[4] This was achieved by amalgamating tribunals by area. The city of Kingston-upon-Hull once had its own tribunal; now one body covers the entire East Riding of Yorkshire, and is administered from Leeds, fifty miles away from Hull. A different policy can be seen in the case of the industrial tribunals set up under the Industrial Training Act of 1964 to hear appeals against assessments of firms for the industrial training levy for their industry, and against the amount of levy imposed. These tribunals were subsequently given other tasks; to hear appeals by dismissed employees against their former employers for redundancy payments under the Redundancy Payments Act of 1965, and to hear appeals by business concerns against their exclusion from the payment of premia under the Selective Employment Payments Act of 1966. The work load of these tribunals was thus considerably increased; the tribunal for the Yorkshire and Humberside region sat once a week in 1964, but now sits daily and has a full-time chairman, a senior barrister who commands a high salary; but the work load is sufficient to require his full-time employment on Tribunal work.

---

[1] Cmnd 218, para. 18.   [2] Cmnd 218, para. 139 and Recommendation 35.
[3] Cmnd 218, para. 139.
[4] Pollard, *op. cit.*, p. 77 and Garner, *op. cit.*, p. 347, n. 3 for these figures.

Nationally, industrial tribunals heard approximately 10,500 redundancy payments cases in 1966, about 2,500 selective employment cases, a similar number of industrial training levy appeals, and some 500 compensation appeals; a considerable volume of work, of a variety of kinds. To give a picture of one industrial tribunal's work, the Yorkshire and Humberside Tribunal hears roughly one-eighth of these cases, amounting to some 1,300 a year about 840 of which are redundancy payments cases. Thus industrial tribunals affect the incomes or business prospects of a sizeable number of people every year.

Rent tribunals deal with some 15,000 cases a year, according to the Franks Committee. Again, to give a picture for one tribunal, the East Yorkshire Rent Tribunal hears about 150 cases a year and sits about once a week, hearing two or three cases at each sitting. A National Insurance local tribunal also sat about once a week,[1] though it heard rather more cases at each sitting; five was roughly the average in this case. On a national scale, however, these tribunals are busier than industrial tribunals; in 1956 their case load was about 43,000 cases, made up as follows:

Unemployment benefit	19,000
Sickness benefit	12,500
Retirement pension	1,700
Industrial injury[2]	7,000[3]

In more recent years the case load was reduced somewhat, it being 41,139 in 1960 and only 36,409 in 1966. Four tribunals were closed between 1961 and 1966, but their number still stands at 200, and the average yearly case load is thus of the order of 180 per tribunal. Again, seen from either the national or the local standpoint, National Insurance local tribunals affect a lot of people's lives each year. In addition to these tribunals, there is a separate system for dealing with claims for industrial injury benefit, consisting of local medical boards, from whose decision an appeal lies to one of fourteen medical appeal tribunals. In 1956, the medical boards dealt with over 300,000 cases, of which 14,500 were appealed to the medical appeal tribunals.[4] One medical

---

[1] Some National Insurance Local Tribunals sit daily.

[2] Only cases concerned with entitlement to benefit go to these tribunals. Assessments are the responsibility of medical boards and medical appeal Tribunals.

[3] Sir G. S. King, *The Ministry of Pensions and National Insurance* (Allen & Unwin, 1958), pp. 86–7.   [4] *Ibid.*

appeal tribunal attended by the author sits daily and hears, on average, twelve cases per session. Between 1962 and 1966 its annual case loads were as follows:

1962	2,216	1965	1,633
1963	1,747	1966	1,554
1964	1,859		

There has been a slight tendency towards a decline in the number of appeals, but their number is still large. National Assistance appeal tribunals, dealing with appeals against refusals to grant National Assistance, against the rate of grant made, or against conditions attached to a grant, are also much used; between 1950 and 1965 there were just over 150 of these tribunals each hearing some seventy cases a year. In the social security field, tribunals are an important part of the administrative machine, arbitrating in countless disputes between authority and the individual, and it would seem that it is therefore of importance that their procedure and operation should be fair and acceptable to those who appear before them. Until 1958 attention was spasmodic, being given only during what Professor Griffith would call one of the battles of administrative justice which broke out from time to time.[1] The sheer size of the task performed by these tribunals is sufficient to make one feel that Professor Griffith was wrong to say that 'the Franks Report and its consequences will be remembered as Old Kaspar remembered the Battle of Blenheim, not indeed for its indiscriminate massacre (the Franks Report rolled no heads) but for the contrast between the noise and tumult of the battle and the relative unimportance of the argument which was its cause'.[2]

In the social security field alone tribunals play a role which is not only of considerable importance in the administration of the benefit schemes, but which also affects many citizens each year where it hurts most—in the pocket. The issues seem of sufficient importance to merit official and public concern.

Apart from the social security tribunals, which are undoubtedly the busiest of all, the tribunal system has been adopted in several other fields. Tribunals sit to hear appeals against proposals to cancel a dairy farmer's registration as such, to consider the enforcement of notices to quit agricultural holdings, and applications for certificates of bad

---

[1] Griffith, *op. cit.*   [2] Griffith, *op.cit.*, p. 145.

husbandry under the Agriculture Acts of 1947 and 1958, and the Agricultural Holdings Act of 1948.[1] The agricultural land tribunals concerned with the last two issues also hear applications by landowners to order a neighbour to clear a ditch whose bad condition is proving a nuisance to them,[2] and have several other responsibilities. The Milk tribunals concerned with dairy farming rarely sit, but agricultural land tribunals are fairly busy, with fairly wide beats to patrol; one tribunal covers Lancashire and the East and West Ridings of Yorkshire, for example. Such a tribunal hears some thirty or forty cases a year on average, though the number may go over fifty on occasion. Besides these tribunals, the Agricultural Holdings Act of 1948 provides for arbitration in such matters as disputes over compensation for repairs done by agricultural tenants, whether by direct payment or by rent reduction. All these tribunals were set up by the Ministry of Agriculture.

In the field of health, too, tribunals are in evidence. Complaints made about treatment or services rendered under the National Health Service by medical, dental, or optical practitioners, or pharmacists, are heard by service committees for each type of practice, appointed by local executive councils. Nationally, there are quite a large number of cases; in 1966 service committees heard 1,006 cases, eighty-five of which resulted in a further appeal to the Minister of Health. Complaints against doctors coming before medical service committees average some 400 a year.[3] There are over 500 service committees, however, and the case load per committee is low; in one city the Executive Council only received one complaint against a doctor in each of the years 1964, 1965 and 1966, plus three against dentists, all received in 1965, and one against a chemist. There were no complaints at all against opticians. In a county area, only three complaints were received between 1962 and 1967, only one of which resulted in a service committee hearing; in the other two, no breach of the practitioner's terms of contract with the service could be discerned, and hence no hearing was necessary. At the local level, the case load is small.[4]

The most controversial tribunals in this field are the mental health review tribunals established under the Mental Health Act of 1959 to

[1] 10 & 11 Geo. 6, ch. 48, 6 & 7 Eliz. 2, ch. 71, 11 & 12 Geo. 6, ch. 63.
[2] Land Drainage Act, 1961, 9 & 10 Eliz. 2, ch. 48.
[3] Reports of the Ministry of Health, 1959–63 (H.M.S.O., 1960–4).
[4] It is of interest that between 1960 and 1966, in some 45 per cent of cases heard the practitioner was found to be in breach of his contract.

hear applications from patients detained compulsorily in mental hospitals, for their release. These tribunals gave rise to anxiety, expressed particularly by the National Council for Civil Liberties, in the early days of their operation, and are concerned with questions of personal liberty in a field where abuse of power is all too easy, since hospital authorities are given wide powers. Between November 1960 and December 1963, 2,600 cases were heard by these tribunals; about 865 a year on average. A local tribunal sits about thirty times a year, hearing one, or occasionally two, cases per sitting. Over time, quite a number of people gain or fail to gain their freedom through proceedings before these tribunals.

Finally, we must mention two tribunals concerned with financial affairs. Valuation courts hear appeals against assessments of gross and rateable value of property made by valuation officers of the Inland Revenue. These courts sit fairly frequently and hear quite a lot of cases; one court visited sits rather more than once a week on average, hearing three or four cases per sitting, though the very existence of the court produces agreed settlements in many cases which never actually come before it. Thus at one sitting, nineteen cases were set down for hearing, but only three were heard; agreement had been reached in the other sixteen, and only formal approval by the court was necessary.

Secondly, there are the General and Special Commissioners of Income Tax, who hear appeals on various aspects of assessment for income tax. Among government departments, the Inland Revenue is among the most uninformative, and little information is forthcoming from them about the work of the Commissioners, but a few years ago, Sir Alexander Johnston was able to reveal that the General and Special Commissioners heard some 8,000 cases a year, about forty of which were appealed to the Chancery Division of the High Court.[1] Again, the number of cases is considerable.

Apart from tribunals, many citizens become involved in public enquiries. The Franks Committee found that planning appeals were running at the rate of some 6,000 a year. More recent figures are somewhat below this; the figures since 1960 are as follows:

1960	4,451	1962	5,361
1961	4,937	1963	5,147

[1] A. Johnston, *The Inland Revenue* (Allen & Unwin, 1965) p. 130.

1964	5,038	1966	4,557
1965	4,368		

There are many other issues where enquiries are required by law, such as railway closures, and compulsory purchase orders; for the latter, the totals for 1960 to 1966 were,

1960	956	1964	1,045
1961	829	1965	1,022
1962	919	1966	874
1963	925		

In these two fields alone, many enquiries are held, each of which may affect the lives and property of several persons. The conclusion we may draw from all these figures must be that tribunals and enquiries play a sizeable part in the administrative process in Britain. It might sometimes appear that their decisions are of no great importance, but this all depends on the point of view. To the administrator dealing in hundreds of millions of pounds, or to the academic observer watching him, a reduction of £10 in rateable value, an increase in a social security benefit of ten shillings a week, or even the compulsory purchase of a cottage for redevelopment, may seem pretty small beer. But to the man in the street, perhaps not well off, perhaps ill or unemployed, or unable to afford expensive housing, these decisions may have a significance sometimes approaching life or death proportions. To him the tribunal or enquiry he attends must seem a vital occasion indeed. To him, it is very important that he should receive justice.

From a discussion of how much work tribunals and enquiries do, we may move on to consider the nature of the tasks they are called upon to undertake. As was mentioned earlier, tribunals are not all called upon to perform the same kind of work. In fact, they range from those whose task it is to apply rules which leave them comparatively little discretion, such as National Assistance local tribunals, whose task is to decide whether insurance officers have correctly applied the rules in refusing benefits, and whose only discretion is in cases in which the rules turn out to be ambiguous (though even then they may be bound by decisions of the Commissioner, which are precedents binding on the tribunals), to tribunals with a range of discretion so wide as to be embarrassing to them.

The contrast will become clearer if we illustrate the work of the various types of tribunals with examples. At one National Insurance tribunal hearing, a person had appealed against refusal of unemployment benefit by an insurance officer on the ground that during the period concerned he had received a payment in lieu of wages. It turned out that in an attempt to do the best they could for an employee of long standing whom they had been forced to dismiss by circumstances beyond their power to rectify, the employers had paid this person a sum which they called an '*ex gratia* payment', instead of the payment of wages in lieu of notice to which he was entitled. Their object in doing this was to enable the dismissed employee to claim unemployment benefit as well, but the tribunal ruled that in view of the claimant's entitlement to wages in lieu of notice, the sum he had received from his former employers must be regarded as a payment in lieu of wages, and therefore as rendering invalid his claim to benefit. The tribunal's task was to interpret the regulations in a case where the employers had attempted to exploit ambiguities. Having decided how the rules applied the tribunal's action was determined; they could only refuse benefit. In another case they held that a man who gave up a job in order to go and live elsewhere, and tried to claim benefit when a job promised him in his new home fell through, was disqualified from receiving benefit for six weeks because he had left his work without sufficient cause. These cases illustrate one type of tribunal work; the interpretation and application of rules.

Another type of tribunal performing similar functions is the industrial tribunal. These were originally set up under the Industrial Training Act of 1964 to hear disputes relating to the Industrial Training Levy, but, as we saw earlier (p. 22), they were allotted a number of other tasks as time went on. The reported cases of these tribunals show that they too are concerned with the interpretation and application of rules and possess only a narrow discretion to interpret the regulations where ambiguity or other difficulties arise. Let us consider two examples which illustrate the kind of decisions these tribunals are called upon to make. The first, the case of East African Standard (Newspapers), Ltd., *v.* Minister of Labour, concerned the selective employment tax.[1] The appellant company published newspapers in Kenya and other parts of

---

[1] *Industrial Tribunals: Reports of Decisions*, ed. Gerald Angel, Barrister at Law, vol. 2, part 5 (H.M.S.O., 1967), pp. 233–6. Source hereafter cited as Angel.

East Africa, and maintained an office in London employing one editorial correspondent and four sales representatives. Under the Selective Employment Payments Act this office had been classified as a 'miscellaneous service' and therefore was held not to qualify for the premium paid to certain classes of industry. The appellants claimed that this office was a part of a newspaper publishing company and should therefore qualify for the premium, but the industrial tribunal hearing the case held that the office could not be so classified since

> the activities of the office are in essence the performance of services for an overseas company, and there is no provision in the Act for payment of a premium or refund to such a company in respect of the employees in an establishment providing such services. The fact that it is a newspaper and publishing company in our view makes no difference. The Standard Industrial Classification[1] applies to industrial activities carried on in Great Britain.

This was a case in which some doubt existed as to the correct classification of the business concerned; the tribunal's task was to decide which view was correct.

The second example will reinforce our view of the work of the industrial tribunals. This is taken from among the cases involving redundancy payments, which now constitute the largest part of the work of these tribunals. In 1966 there occurred two closely related cases, both concerned with the length of service upon which a redundancy payment was to be calculated. The first case was that of Tervitt *v.* West Lothian Steel Foundry Ltd. The applicant had previously been dismissed by the respondents on 18 March 1963, through a shortage of work, and had been re-engaged five weeks later; the question was whether the break was such that the applicant's payment could only be calculated from the date of his reinstatement, or whether the whole of his service with the respondent company should be included. The tribunal ruled that 'while . . . the Redundancy Payments Act of 1965 would probably have allowed a four-week interval (or less) between dismissal and re-engagement by the same employer not to be regarded as breaking the continuity of his period of employment, that would not cover a break (such as in this case) of more than four weeks'.[2]

---

[1] The Standard Industrial Classification is the basis on which firms are divided for the purpose of determining whether they qualify for the refund.
[2] Angel, pp. 253–5.

The second case, that of Gray *v.* Burntisland Shipbuilding Company concerned an employee dismissed and re-engaged after only three weeks, in which the tribunal held that the period of the break in continuity was so short that no break in the length of service upon which his redundancy payment was to be calculated existed under the terms of the Act; he received full payment.[1] The tribunal's duty had been to establish the facts, and then to interpret and apply the rules.

In contrast to these, some tribunals have a discretion so wide as to constitute a virtual *carte blanche*. Rent tribunals, and rent officers and rent assessment committees, are charged to determine a 'fair rent' for premises in cases coming before them. They are given some guidelines; for example, the Rent Act of 1965 lays down that the rent officer and rent assessment committees shall not take scarcity of accommodation into account when assessing fair rents, but their discretion is still very large. Similarly, the Air Transport Licensing Board is given the duty of regulating competition among air lines in this country in the best interests of the public; it is left to the Board to determine what these interests are. The discretion is so wide that these tribunals are, in effect, policy-making bodies, rather than administrative or even judicial. Questions of what constitutes a fair rent or fair and desirable competition are not decided by reference to rules; they are values which those hearing the case must to a large extent promulgate themselves. This can cause difficulties to the tribunals. They are exposed to attack for their decisions in a way that those tribunals which apply rules are not. The Air Transport Licensing Board is most unpopular with the airlines and, moreover, often gets a very bad press. Tribunals concerned with rents too come in for their share of criticism. Left-wing members of parliament mounted an attack on the rent assessment committee set up under the 1965 Rent Act to hear cases involving unfurnished accommodation, for not reducing rents frequently enough; they saw the committees as part of a crusade against the evil landlords and felt that they were not fighting bravely enough. Landlords too are not without bitterness; one, invited to write for a student newspaper on the tribunal system, said:

> Many property-owners I know are rapidly selling investment properties because of the Rent Act, for the simple reasons that they are

[1] Angel, pp. 255–7.

losing money! Thus we have a situation where a piece of legislation designed to help the tenant is having a dangerous long-term effect. It is fast reducing the availability of rented accommodation.[1]

Thus the tribunals are caught in a cross-fire of criticism, always an unpleasant feeling, but probably an inevitable burden for what are virtually independent policy-making bodies.

Furthermore, one may have doubts as to how suitable tribunals are in such fields. Because they have such a wide area of discretion, tribunal judgments may become inconsistent and even arbitrary. For example, when the Council on Tribunals sent a questionnaire to the chairmen of rent tribunals to discover various facts about their procedure, they discovered that the various tribunals had evolved different methods of assessing rents; the majority favoured variations and sometimes combinations of three methods. The first was to take the gross annual value of the property, allot a proportion of this to the letting in question according to the amount of the property involved, and multiply this by an agreed mathematical factor, allowing a reasonable profit on furniture and services provided. A second method was to allot a fixed percentage of the capital value and add an allowance for profit, and the third was to ascertain the unfurnished letting value in the light of comparable lettings and the tribunal's previous decisions, considering also the amount of overcrowding and the general amenities of the district, and then to add to this an allowance for the furniture and services provided. The first method was favoured, in the main, for old property, the second method for new, but each tribunal could and did indulge in its own combinations and permutations of these and other methods.[2] If this was not enough, circumstances might, in the tribunal's eyes, justify a variation of the rent reached by whatever method was adopted.

Now, while it might be argued that consistency is neither possible nor desirable in the case of rent tribunals, such diverse methods of reaching a decision must give rise to concern. It means that, were two identical cases to occur in areas covered by different tribunals (most unlikely, but not impossible), a different rent would very probably be arrived at in each case. The variety of methods used to assess rents

[1] *Torchlight* (University of Hull newspaper), May 1967.
[2] *Third Report of the Council on Tribunals*, 1961 (H.M.S.O., 1962), para. 49.

make such an occurrence not only likely, but highly probable; one may doubt the fairness of such a system.

Between these extreme cases lie tribunals who are given rules to apply but whose discretion is wider than that of National Insurance or Industrial tribunals, such that they have some policy function of the kind given with such prodigal generosity to rent tribunals and the Air Transport Licensing Board; it is, perhaps, not entirely inappropriate that appeals from the latter's decisions go to a Minister[1] and not to a higher tribunal or court. Agricultural land tribunals, for example, appear at first sight to be interpreting rules; when considering whether to confirm a landlord's notice to quit, they must decide whether the landlord has proved his case in terms of one or more explicit provisions of the Agriculture Acts of 1947 and 1958. These are that the eviction is in the interests of good husbandry, or good estate management; that the eviction is desirable for the pursuance of agricultural research, education, experiment, demonstration, or in order that the land may be used for smallholdings or allotments. The landlord may also seek to prove that greater hardship will result to him if the notice is not enforced than will result to the tenant if it is. Finally, an eviction may be sought to allow the land to be used for purposes other than agriculture.[2] If this were all, the tribunals would be fairly closely bound by the rules laid down and would only have to determine the facts and apply them; but this section of the 1958 Act, having stated the five conditions, ends with the following words: 'Provided that, notwithstanding that they are satisfied as aforesaid, the tribunal shall withhold consent to the operation of the notice to quit if in all the circumstances it appears to them that a fair and reasonable landlord would not insist on possession.' This gives the tribunals a discretion; they have to decide what would be 'fair and reasonable' for a landlord to do in the circumstances before them. This discretion is similar to that given to the Restrictive Practices Court by Section 21 of the Restrictive Trade Practices Act of 1956[3] which lays down seven possible ways in which a restrictive practice may be justified before the Court; the so-called 'gateways' through which a practice may pass to legitimacy, and closes by enjoining the Court to satisfy itself further that 'the restriction is not

[1] Now the President of the Board of Trade.
[2] Agriculture Act 1958, Section 1.   [3] 4 & 5 Eliz. 2, ch. 68.

unreasonable having regard to the balance between those circumstances[1] and any detriment to the public or to persons not parties to the agreement . . . resulting or likely to result from the operation of the restriction'. Both the Restrictive Practices Court and agricultural land tribunals are thus given a wide discretion which makes them to a degree policy-making rather than rule-applying bodies, and neither is therefore a tribunal in the sense described by the Franks Committee.

There are other tribunals which cannot be said simply to apply rules. Valuation courts, for example, have to decide how much, in terms of rateable value, an unpleasant smell, excessive noise, an unsightly development or the proximity of a prison or mental asylum is worth, a discretion similar to that given to rent tribunals. Thus there are many degrees of discretion given to tribunals. Some apply rules; others have to make decisions in which value judgments must play a major part.

Public enquiries, for their part, are never specifically concerned with the application of rules; they are supposed simply to collect information and, in the words of Lord Thankerton, giving judgment in the Stevenage case, 'to inform the mind of the Minister'. The kind of question an enquiry may be called upon to consider, to cite an actual issue, is whether a smelting firm should be allowed to build a chimney near an aerodrome used both for a public service and for testing new aircraft built by the company who owned it. The chimney would put an end to plans to expand the airfield for more commercial use, and indeed would virtually terminate its usefulness as a civil airport; on the other hand, failure to allow the chimney would, it was claimed, seriously damage and perhaps destroy an industrial concern important both to the local and to the national economy. Ultimately, the civil servant who decided was making a choice of considerable importance in which there were no rules to guide him; he had to weigh the contentions of the warring interests and decide which had to be given the victory. Again, a public enquiry may oblige the person charged with making the decisions to decide whether the need for petrol stations or the need for unspoilt countryside shall prevail. But such duties are not different in kind from those imposed on many tribunals, such as rent tribunals, the Air Transport Licensing Board and, to a lesser degree,

---

[1] i.e. the circumstances justifying the agreement's retention via one or more 'gateways'.

those of agricultural land tribunals, or even the Restrictive Practices Court. The differences are of degree, not of kind, and the extent to which administrative tribunals and enquiries are called upon to exercise a discretion varies right across the field.

III PROCEDURE AND PERSONNEL

Apart from the need for just laws, the polity demands able and disinterested administration of those laws. As J. R. Lucas has written:

> ... no set of laws that are complete and perfectly precise has ever yet been formulated, nor is it likely to be. We are able to make any point clear, but we cannot make every point clear. Any particular set of circumstances may be considered and a decision for those circumstances given, but no formula can be constructed that will unambiguously cover all sets of circumstances. And therefore we need judges, to decide difficult cases which cannot always be straightforwardly subsumed under general principles, but call for some measure of judgement. The common saying that government should be a government of laws, not men, cannot be completely realised. We always need some men, judges, to say what the law is, and although we may demand that they be not arbitrary in their judgements but observe principles, we cannot tie them down completely, and completely specify the principles, except as being what the judges say they are.[1]

If justice is to be achieved, these judges must observe certain standards of probity and objectivity. No man should be judge in his own cause, no party should be condemned unheard, no party should be heard in the absence of the other parties, all should know the case they will have to meet before the hearing, and the judges should give with their decisions the reasons which have led them to them. Thus we can seek to ensure that judges are objective, and that all the facts of the case are laid before them. Against these standards, administrative tribunals and enquiries have often been measured, and sometimes found wanting, and in the light of these principles proposals for their reform have been made both officially and unofficially; officially by the Donoughmore and Franks Committees, unofficially, by Professor W. A. Robson and others. It is with the first four of these principles that we are concerned in the present chapter; they all relate to procedure and personnel.

[1] J. R. Lucas, *The Principles of Politics* (O.U.P., 1966), pp. 25-6.

The first principle, that no man should be judge in his own cause, brings us at once to the question of the appointment of chairmen and members of tribunals. To ensure objectivity, the Franks Committee recommended that tribunal chairmen should be appointed by the Lord Chancellor, and to ensure that they would be capable of organising a fair procedure, they recommended that chairmen should have legal qualifications and experience.[1] In many cases, these recommendations have been followed. Of the tribunals investigated in the present study, only one did not have a lawyer chairman, the Valuation Courts hearing appeals against assessments for rates. In these courts the chairmen are appointed by the local authorities concerned under schemes agreed between the authorities in each court's area. The authorities and a representative of the Ministry of Housing and Local Government meet and confer, after which the agreed scheme for appointment to the court is enacted by the Minister. In the case of five other tribunals, the chairman was appointed by the Lord Chancellor, though in the other five cases the Minister of the Department concerned still makes the appointments and is thus still to some extent judge in his own cause, although in all these cases lawyer chairmen are required.

In the case of tribunal members, other needs are recognised. First, much of the subject-matter of tribunal proceedings demands expert consideration. No layman could be expected to pronounce with authority on many medical questions, such as whether a particular symptom could have been the result of an industrial accident, the chief issue for medical boards and medical appeal tribunals. Both these tribunals therefore have medical members; indeed, the medical boards consist entirely of medical men, though the appellate tribunals have lawyer chairmen, assisted by two specialists of consultant rank; the Ministry of Social Security tries to ensure that one of these medical members specialises in a field appropriate to the majority of the cases coming before the tribunals; orthopaedists are in demand in mining or dock areas, for example.

Secondly, the tribunals may be concerned with the reconciling of conflicting interests, which may be represented in the decision-making process to see that fair play is done. One way in which this is often done is to select tribunal members from interest groups whose members may be involved in the cases coming before the tribunals. This is often

[1] Cmnd 218, Recommendations 2 and 4.

done in the industrial field in particular, where tribunal members are chosen as representatives of employers and employed. The industrial tribunals set up under the Industrial Training Act of 1964 to adjudicate in disputes as to whether a firm is liable for the industrial training levy imposed for a particular industry, whose jurisdiction has subsequently been extended to cover questions of eligibility for refunds of the selective employment tax, of the entitlement of dismissed employees to redundancy payments, and certain other compensation questions, provide a good example. The matters coming before these tribunals for decision affect both 'sides' of industry, and their members are chosen by the Minister of Labour from among representatives of employers and representatives of organised labour. Often, persons with an interest at stake in a particular field are also knowledgeable about that field and are therefore able to supply expertise as well as being representatives of their fellows.

In the appointment of tribunal members, interest groups frequently play an important role. It is part of the process described by Professor S. E. Finer whereby interest groups are drawn into Government administration under the pressure of mutual need.[1] In this case, the government departments need men with both expertise and a position that will convince persons appearing before the tribunals that their interests have an advocate on the 'Bench', so to speak; that they will get a fair deal, and render it more likely that parties will accept the tribunals' decisions as reasonable. The interest groups, for their part, wish to ensure by all possible means that their members get good treatment. Hence they collaborate willingly in the appointment from their ranks of tribunal members.

A type of procedure frequently used is that existing in the case of the National Insurance local tribunals. The National Insurance Advisory Committee prepares a list of approved employers' and workpeople's organisations who are each invited to nominate one or two members to panels from whom tribunal members will be selected in rotation, one at a time from each panel. Before admission to the panels, the proposed names are submitted to the Advisory Committee for approval, after which the persons concerned are interviewed by the district officer of the Ministry of Social Security to ensure that they are sufficiently educated, intelligent and honest for the job. Thus organisations and

[1] S. E. Finer, *Anonymous Empire* (Pall Mall paper edn, 1966), ch. 4.

D

individuals are carefully screened so that only responsible persons and organisations take part, a point which also emerges in Professor Finer's study of the process whereby information and consents flow from pressure groups to Whitehall.[1] The Ministry do have some say in the appointment of members, however, which is not entirely desirable.

A similar system operates in the case of agricultural land tribunals, which have to arbitrate between landlords and tenant farmers in such matters as proposals to evict tenants, proceedings to obtain a certificate of bad husbandry against a tenant, or to enforce legitimate demands from tenants for landlords to make improvements to their holdings. The constituting statute lays down that the members of the tribunals must be members of panels selected by the Minister of Agriculture from among persons 'appearing to the Minister to represent' the interests of landlords and farmers.[2] In fact, these panels are chosen from persons nominated by the County Landowners' Association and the National Farmers' Union. The Minister has made use of the interest groups to determine who represents the interests of farmers and those of landlords. It is another example of a Minister seeking, and getting, the assistance of interest groups in carrying out his responsibilities as prescribed by statute. The Minister gets members of affected groups of persons to act as judges in cases affecting their fellows; it is an excellent example of Professor John Rawls' idea of a community of self-interested individuals controlling one another's practices;[3] a settlement acceptable to all and abhorrent or unduly advantageous to none should emerge.

The most difficult problem of all in this matter of who is to decide cases is presented by public enquiries. These are conducted by inspectors on the staff of the Ministries concerned, who hear the parties but do not themselves decide the issues. Their task is to report on the evidence, in theory to the Minister, but in fact to one of a group of civil servants charged with deciding enquiry cases, such as the Appeals Division of the Ministry of Housing and Local Government, who then take the decision on the basis of the inspector's report plus whatever other information they may choose to consider. This system has often come in for criticism. The Donoughmore Committee, commenting on it, declared

1 S. E. Finer, *Anonymous Empire*, (Pall Mall paper edn, 1966), chap. 4. pp. 33–4.
2 Agriculture Act 1947, Ninth Schedule, para. 15.
3 J. Rawls, 'Justice as Fairness', in *Philosophical Review*, 1958, Section 3.

that 'bias from strong and sincere conviction as to public policy may operate as a more serious disqualification than pecuniary interest',[1] thereby putting public policy on a level with such disqualifications from the judgment seat as financial or proprietary interest. Again, Professor H. W. R. Wade, asking the question, 'Are Public Enquiries a Farce?' in 1954, wrote that 'the usual complaint is that the Minister is ... prosecutor, judge and jury in his own case, and ... it is too much to expect the objections to be given fair weight'.[2] However, it is not as simple as this. Professor S. A. de Smith pointed out that 'the Minister is responsible for the co-ordination of overall planning policy' in the case of planning appeals.[3] The Minister and his policy must have a *locus standi* in the decision-making process, just as must the views of the citizen, otherwise the decisions of arbitrators could disrupt and even destroy ministerial policy willy-nilly. In any case, the Ministry holding the enquiry is often not deeply involved in the issues in dispute; most public enquiries are held as a result of appeals from decisions or proposals of local authorities, such as compulsory purchase orders or refusals by local authorities of planning permission for development, and the Minister is called upon to arbitrate between the citizen and his local council. Sometimes the dispute may in fact be chiefly between rival private interests. An enquiry held recently was concerned with the proposal of a smelting company to erect a 600 foot high chimney at their works near an aircraft factory which possessed an airstrip used for an internal air service, and which it was proposed to extend to allow the use of larger airliners on the route. The plans of the two firms were incompatible, since the erection of the chimney would render the airstrip too dangerous for large commercial aircraft, while the smelting firm claimed that they would have to cease operations on their site unless they could use new techniques for which the chimney was essential. The planning authority refused permission, and it fell to the Ministry of Housing and Local Government to decide, amidst accusation and counter-accusation of selfishness and unconcern with the national interest, whose interests should prevail. Other government departments were involved; the Board of Trade, as the department responsible both for airports and for industry, was in a dilemma, while the Ministry of Defence were concerned about an important aircraft factory, but the

[1] Cmnd 4060, Section III, para. 3.
[2] *Public Administration*, 1955, pp. 390–1.   [3] Pollard, *op. cit.*, p. 114.

Ministry hearing the appeal was not involved in the dispute. In other cases, however, a department may be more intimately involved, as where the Ministry of Transport hears objections to the proposed route of a new motorway which it has itself drawn up. Local officials may endeavour to involve the Ministry and its officials by attempting to show that their proposals are concerned with the execution of ministerial policy; thus in an enquiry concerned with new parking restrictions proposed for a country town, the Town Clerk and the Borough Engineer referred on several occasions to Ministry circulars with which they claimed the Borough authority were attempting to comply. The latter officer, after pointing out that 90 per cent of the traffic using the town centre was local in origin and destination, went on to say:

> To meet this situation the Council have requested that the approved Town Map should be amended by the addition of a number of new roads but since the construction of these must of necessity be phased over a number of years, it is essential that the existing street pattern is used to its best advantage if complete congestion is to be avoided. *This is in accordance with the principles set out in Ministry of Transport Circulars 1/64 and 1/65.*[1]

In such cases, the Ministry is to some degree judge in its own cause, although since the Ministry is charged with the responsibility for national policy and must be able effectively to discharge that responsibility, this is not necessarily an illegitimate distribution of power. Nonetheless, as the Franks Committee recognised, the degree of involvement of the deciding Ministry varies from case to case, even though all enquiry proposals 'involve the weighing of proposals, or decisions, or provisional proposals or decisions, made by a public authority on the one hand against the views and interests of those affected by them of the other'.[2] Our examples show how the degree of ministerial involvement can differ.

The motives of objectors at public enquiries can differ widely, too. Understandably, perhaps, selfish considerations may not be entirely absent from their minds though they may not be the sole or even the dominant motives behind objections; as Denys Munby put it:

> Though most of the objectors may . . . be property owners whose property is liable for designation for compulsory purchase, societies

---

[1] My italics.   [2] Cmnd 218, paras. 266–7.

concerned for amenities and others interested in the proper planning of their local areas also take part. . . . In so far as the purpose of public enquiries is to bring to light all the facts and ensure full publicity for alternative proposals, it is these objectors who merit the greater attention rather than those who are merely concerned that a particular school or housing scheme should be sited on their neighbours' land rather than their own.[1]

Objectors' motives vary from the purely selfish to a genuine concern that the public should get the best possible amenities in the most economical way. Someone must not only weigh the relative importance of the arguments advanced at the enquiry, but must also assess the needs of public policy. An independent arbitrator might well find himself in a position where he had either to support or to obstruct ministerial policy; he will become involved in political decisions and his position would become somewhat akin to that of the Supreme Court of the United States where a Court decision will result in the annulment of a Congressional statute and bring it into conflict with Congress and the Administration, as happened in the 'New Deal' cases in 1936–7. To avoid such a conflict, and to ensure that adjudicators cannot vitiate ministerial policy, for which the Minister is in any case accountable in the High Court of Parliament, it is desirable that the person who decides the cases should be part of the department concerned. As things are at present, a special section is usually responsible for these decisions, so that at least they are taken in an arena separate from the other work of the department.

Such, then, is the composition of tribunals and enquiries at present. Since the passing of the 1958 Act appointment of chairmen has become generally the responsibility of the Lord Chancellor rather than of departmental Ministers, as was the case previously. In some cases, the change was made by legislation; for example, in 1959 appointment to National Assistance appeal tribunals was transferred from the Minister of Pensions and National Insurance to the Lord Chancellor.[2] Tribunals set up since 1958 have been constituted in conformity with the recommendations of the Franks Committee, and in any case, the 1958

---

[1] *Public Administration*, 1956, p. 181.
[2] Report of the National Assistance Board for 1959, Cmnd 1085. (H.M.S.O., 1960).

Act requires that new rules for tribunal proceedings shall be promulgated only after consultation with the Council on Tribunals. Chairmen
and members of mental health review tribunals, which were set up
under the Mental Health Act of 1959,[1] are appointed by the Lord
Chancellor as are chairmen of industrial tribunals. This is a considerable change compared with the findings of Robert Pollard and his
colleagues in the late nineteen-forties, that of the nine tribunals investigated, all but one had chairmen appointed by the Minister concerned
in the cases heard,[2] the exception being valuation courts, where the
appointments were, and still are, made by county or county borough
authorities, which means that in the counties the rating authorities do
not make the appointments, though they do in the single-tier county
boroughs. While one could approve of declarations of virtue such as
the following, made by the National Assistance Board in 1935, that in
appointing tribunal chairmen, 'the main qualifications looked for by
the Minister . . . were knowledge of local conditions, good local standing, and ability to conduct the proceedings of appeal with thoroughness,
impartiality, and dispatch',[3] one cannot help feeling that appointments
made by a department not involved in the issues coming before the
tribunals, such as the Lord Chancellor's Office, is an improvement as
far as the demand that 'no man shall be judge in his own cause' is concerned, although it does mean a considerable increase in work for that
department, whose selections of judicial officers may not always be
above reproach, as recent criticism of magistrates' courts suggests;[4]
with the increase in work there is a danger that appointments of tribunal
chairmen will be made in haste without sufficient scrutiny of the candi-
dates. However, if complaints arise about a particular tribunal, and
these are brought to the notice of the Council on Tribunals, the
Council will bring these to the Lord Chancellor's notice, and he is
empowered to take remedial steps, up to the removal of chairmen
who are found wanting.[5]

Before leaving the composition of tribunals, we ought to consider
the status and work of tribunal clerks. With the exception of clerks to
valuation courts, who are chosen by the courts they serve and are paid

---

[1] 7 & 8 Eliz. 2, ch. 72.   [2] Pollard, *op. cit.*, various.
[3] Report of the National Assistance Board for 1935, Cmd 5177 (H.M.S.O.,
1936), p. 49.
[4] See R. Hood, *Sentencing in Magistrates' Courts* (Stevens, 1962).
[5] Tribunals and Enquiries Act 1958, Section 3, para. 8(c).

by the Ministry of Housing and Local Government, and the clerks to the General Commissioners of Income Tax, who are also chosen by the bodies they serve, tribunals are serviced by civil service staff, from the Ministry to which their work appertains. This has proved to be administratively the simplest solution, and because other solutions suggested to the Franks Committee would raise great difficulties, in the Committee's view, they felt that this form of servicing should continue. They gave 'careful consideration' to the establishment of an independent staff of tribunal clerks under the Lord Chancellor's supervision, but rejected the proposal, saying that within such a staff there could be no career structure attractive enough to attract good recruits, it would be difficult to keep the clerks fully occupied and free from conflicting appointments, and lastly that it would mean the end of a training scheme for staff operated by the social service departments, whereby staff acted as tribunal clerks for a period to gain experience of the tribunals' work—a scheme, said the Committee, 'which is doubtless valuable in developing the outlook appropriate to the administration of a social service'.[1] However, they enjoined the proposed Council on Tribunals to keep a careful watch on the activities of clerks:

> In order to ensure that departmental clerks cannot exercise a departmental influence upon tribunals, we regard it as essential that their duties and conduct should be regulated on the advice of the Council on Tribunals. The general principles to be followed are that the duties of a clerk should be confined to secretarial work, the taking of such notes of evidence as may be required, and the tendering of advice, when requested, on points connected with the tribunal's functions. Like a magistrates' clerk he should be debarred from retiring with the tribunal when they consider their decision unless he is sent for to advise on a specific point.[2]

In general, clerks do seem to confine themselves to the duties here laid down, although not infrequently they remain with the tribunals while the latter discuss their decision; where departmental clerks were employed, however, this practice was less frequent. In many cases, mainly because of the nature of the accommodation provided for the tribunal, the applicant citizen and the other party were asked to withdraw from the room, with any other member of the public who was present,

[1] Cmnd 218, para. 60.   [2] Cmnd 218, para. 61.

while leaving tribunal and clerk together in the hearing room. The importance of this may vary according to the kind of work the tribunal is doing; this practice was resorted to at the medical appeal tribunals attended, but as the cases are highly specialised and the final decision must largely be that of the expert medical members, the presence or absence of the clerk is relatively unimportant. In other fields, where less expertise is required, the clerk's presence at the tribunal's deliberations might give rise to suspicion as to his part in the proceedings, and this should be avoided if at all possible. In the main, though, clerks confine themselves to dealing with the applications for hearings, booking accommodation, listing cases for hearing and notifying the parties, assembling tribunal members and recording the proceedings and decisions. One industrial tribunal had resorted to automation in the form of a dictaphone into which the chairman read his statement of the tribunal's decision and reasons, to be copied later. Most clerks are established civil servants, though rent tribunal clerks are not established, and their position has aroused some concern; one of the Council on Tribunals' first achievements was to secure an improvement in the status of these clerks.[1]

One area where concern has been expressed about the position of the tribunal clerks is National Assistance. Not only have the clerks frequently retired with the tribunals; they are also senior officials of the Ministry of Social Security (formerly of the National Assistance Board), rather than junior clerical staff, as with most other tribunals. When George Lach wrote his essay in the Pollard symposium, he was able to disclose that these clerks were Assistant District Officers originally, and that when the Districts were abolished the clerks were still officials of rank higher than that of the Area Officers who gave the original decision on benefit claims.[2] Mr Lach felt that so senior an official might be able to carry a good deal of weight with the tribunal and hence unduly influence its decisions, especially if he remained with the members when they retired. As early as 1929 a committee under the chairmanship of Sir Harold Morris, K.C., commented on the National Assistance Appeal Board clerks and issued a firm injunction to the civil servants to mend their ways:

The Court . . . will require an officer as clerk, but his duties should

[1] First Report, 1959 (H.M.S.O., 1960), para. 93.   [2] Pollard, *op cit.*, p. 48.

be strictly confined to those of arranging the papers for the Court, recording decisions, and communicating them to claimants, and the other formal duties necessarily appended to the work of a Court. We have evidence that in some cases, after the claimant has withdrawn, the appeals officers remained whilst the Court were discussing their decision. . . . All persons, other than the chairman and the members, should withdraw while the scope of the decision is being discussed.[1]

Writing nearly twenty years after this report, Mr Lach also felt concern at the conduct of these tribunals. Because the clerks were so senior, he felt, they tended to take an active part in the proceedings, and there was a tendency for the tribunal to lean on the clerk for advice when a case was proving difficult. What was more, being a man both in and under authority, so to speak, the clerk might either be the officer who had given the original decision, or he might be under the supervision of a more senior official whose decisions or policy might be in question before the tribunal. Given his position and freedom to intervene, undue influence might result; Mr Lach said that 'the pressure operating on the clerk when decisions of his senior officers were before appeal tribunals and the clerk's pressure on the tribunal to uphold their decision can be imagined'.[2] The problem has continued to exercise the minds of those concerned with ensuring justice in the administrative field; the Franks Committee did not comment on the activities of National Assistance appeal tribunal clerks, but the Council on Tribunals has had some critical things to say. In their second report they remark that 'in the case of [National Assistance] Tribunals, we felt that the clerk was permitted by the Chairmen to take too active a part in the proceedings'.[3] This is a problem which the Council is still watching with special attention. When asked about the present position, the Ministry proved completely uncommunicative.

In the case of National Insurance local tribunals also the activities of the clerks has attracted the Council's attention; they found out that the clerk 'normally remains with the tribunal when they are considering their decision'[4] and also complained that they were unable to perform the duty laid upon them of supervising the working of these tribunals

[1] Cmd 3415, p. 70. [2] Pollard, *op. cit.*, p. 60.
[3] Second Report, 1960 (H.M.S.O., 1961), para. 53.
[4] Fourth Report, 1962 (H.M.S.O., 1963), para. 21.

since the regulations governing their proceedings forbade chairmen
to invite outside persons to retire with the tribunals; clerical influence
could not be checked. It took the Council three years' agitation to
obtain even a promise from the Minister that this ban would be ended.[1]
At the tribunals attended by the present author, the clerks did remain
in the room while the tribunal discussed their decision; additional
evidence was furnished by an indignant citizen who wrote in his local
newspaper that:

> The proceedings [of the National Insurance tribunal] were cosy and
> courteous in the smooth English way, but quite undemocratic. I
> was asked a few questions about dates by the chairman, but not
> invited to state the reasons for my appeal.
>
> I was then excluded from the room while, as I presumed, the
> insurance officer put in his fourpence-worth. Later a clerk told me
> that my appeal had been disallowed.[2]

The implication of this is that not only the clerk, but also the insurance
officer, remained with the tribunal in this particular case, while the
claimant was excluded, and while not wishing to imply that proceedings before these tribunals are actually unfair, such practices cannot
but undermine public confidence in them. In the case of National
Assistance tribunals, Mr Lach pointed out that few claimants ever
appealed to the tribunals; only 0·39 per cent of claimants appealed,
and even this is an overestimate of the proportion appealing, since
every change in a recipient's circumstances requires a new assessment
and gives rise to a new opportunity to appeal, so that 0·39 per cent is,
if anything, too high an estimate. This trend has continued; between
1949 and 1965 only 0·42 per cent of fresh claimants appealed.[3] This
may be a tribute to the justness of the decisions of the Board's officers;
equally, it might be an indication of lack of confidence in the appeal
system. Certainly, as we have seen, the activities of some tribunal
clerks is not calculated to reassure the public, and it is impossible either
to verify or falsify suspicions aroused, because a veil of secrecy sur-
rounds these tribunals. On the other hand, speaking more generally,
it must be said that in no tribunal actually investigated in the present

[1] Seventh Report, 1965 (H.M.S.O., 1966), para. 6.
[2] *Shropshire Star*, 18 July, 1967.
[3] Reports of the National Assistance Board, 1949–65 (H.M.S.O., 1950–66).

study did a Departmental clerk appear to play an unduly large part in the proceedings; they confined themselves to supplying documents or information to the Chairman when asked to do so, and to keeping a record of the proceedings and decisions. The Council on Tribunals receive few complaints about clerks; in the main they confine themselves to secretarial duties, and only occasionally do their actions give rise to suspicion on the part of the public or the Council. Much depends on the chairmen of tribunals, as we shall see in discussing procedure, a discussion to which we must now turn.

The rules of natural justice demand that both parties to any proceedings should be heard; the rule of *audi alterem partem*; further demands often made are that they should be heard in each other's presence, that each party should have an opportunity to question the other and to cross-examine opposing witnesses. Also, hearings must be well-ordered. Cases must be presented coherently if the tribunal is to have a clear view of the arguments and evidence presented by each side in support of its case, and disorder can rapidly degenerate into chaos, especially if feelings between the parties are running high. One tribunal hearing degenerated into a shouting match for a time because the chairman failed to keep a firm hand on the proceedings. Again, one medical appeal tribunal clerk said that his tribunal refrained from announcing its decisions orally because unsuccessful appellants would often start shouting and swearing at the tribunal when their defeat was announced. But thirdly, in a field where legal or other representation is not common, and where members of the public appearing before the tribunals tend to be poorly educated, incoherent, scared, or all three together, there is need for a form of procedure which is at once orderly and reassuring to the citizen, and which gives him the best possible chance to present his case. Unless the private citizen is represented, tribunal proceedings often inevitably become something of a David and Goliath contest. Writing on planning enquiries, Professor S. A. de Smith recalled an objector, under cross-examination by a prominent Q.C. briefed by a wealthy local authority, who said in desperation that 'You must bear in mind, Sir, that this is the first time I've ever been in a place like this, and I'm absolutely lost',[1] and even though government departments and local authorities rarely if ever brief counsel or solicitors to appear on their behalf in tribunal proceedings, the officials who

[1] Pollard, *op. cit.*, p. 109.

do so appear acquire experience in presenting cases, experience which the private citizen almost always lacks completely. The proceedings must therefore be so conducted that he will not be overawed, and should if possible be designed to assist him in presenting his arguments and so reduce the odds against him. We shall consider the problems raised by advocacy before administrative bodies in the next chapter; for the moment we are concerned with advocacy only in so far as it affects the conduct of proceedings.

Procedure at administrative tribunals is, perhaps, more uniform than might be expected. It is based on the procedure of magistrates' courts, though chairmen are usually given a wide discretion to conduct hearings as they think fit. At medical appeal tribunals, as with several others, procedure is entirely at the chairman's discretion. If the tribunal is empowered to administer the oath, it is for the chairman to decide whether to do so; most tribunals are so empowered today, though at most the power is seldom used. One agricultural land tribunal chairman always orders the oath to be administered, as a matter of course, but of the tribunals visited this was the only one where the oath was administered, though at one industrial tribunal the chairman asked parties presenting witnesses whether they wished their witnesses to take the oath.

Where there is a further appeal from the decision of a tribunal, whether to a court of law or to a superior administrative body, such as the National Insurance Commissioner, appeal decisions often lay down that certain procedural features must be present at any hearing in the inferior tribunals. In the case of medical appeal tribunals, for example, where there is an appeal to the Commissioner on points of law, the Commissioner has determined that appellants shall always be invited to comment on the evidence presented to the tribunals by the insurance officer and by his own representative, if he has one. Another decision prescribes that the appellant or his representative must be permitted to see all documents presented in evidence by the Ministry. Apart from such appeals, there are the ancient High Court powers of prohibition, *certiorari*, and *mandamus*.[1] The citizen may apply for a

---

[1] There is also a more modern remedy, that of Declaration, which is more effective and more widely applicable. Cf. H. W. R. Wade, *Administrative Law*, pp. 128–9, and Barnard *v.* National Dock Labour Board ((1953) 2 Q.B. 18). Giving judgment in this case, Lord Denning pointed out that while tribunals must act

writ to remove a decision to the High Court to be quashed on the grounds that the decision was *ultra vires*, or that the procedure was improper or unjust. It is an unwieldy procedure, seldom used and still more rarely successful, for the doctrine expounded by the House of Lords in Arlidge's case[1] makes it difficult to attack administrative procedures through the courts, since it was laid down in the judgment in this case that many legal standards of procedure are inapplicable to administrative proceedings. The Franks Committee, however, thought that these powers should be retained, and should be strengthened by providing for an appeal to the courts on points of law where no right of appeal to another tribunal existed.[2] In a number of cases, such a provision now exists, as in the case of the industrial tribunals, from whose decisions an appeal lies to the High Court on points of law. One such appeal was made in 1966 against a tribunal's definition of redundancy under the Redundancy Payments Act 1965, when the High Court ruled that the tribunal were in error because 'they have not looked at the overall requirements of the business' for a particular type of labour; if this were unchanged, even though the duties assigned to a particular post had been changed, a dismissal arising from this could not be described for the purposes of claiming a payment as resulting from redundancy; in the case in question, it was held that the appellant had been unable to meet the standards now required of him, and had been dismissed for this reason.[3] Where such an appeal as this is provided for, it can to some extent act as a check on procedure, though only in so far as procedure is laid down by law; if, as is usually the case, procedure is at the discretion of the chairman, only the remedies of prohibition, *mandamus* and *certiorari* remain.

A further check on procedure, however, is furnished by the Council

---

according to the law, if complainants resorted to *certiorari*, they would probably fail, in view of the limitations imposed on this remedy by the courts: indeed, the applicant in Barnard's case would have failed. Hence it was desirable that the more flexible remedy of declaration should be available, by which, it seemed, almost any decision could be attacked. Lord Denning asked 'Why . . . should the Court not intervene by declaration and injunction? If it cannot so intervene, it would mean that the tribunal could disregard the law, which is a thing no-one can do in this country', thus seeming to give the remedy of Declaration a broad coverage denied to the remedies of prohibition, *certiorari*, or *mandamus*.

[1] See pp. 2–3 above.
[2] Cmnd 218, paras. 107–9 and Recommendation 27.
[3] North Riding Garages Ltd *v.* Butterwick, Angel, pp. 229–33.

on Tribunals, both by members' visits to tribunals and by the right of
members of the public to complain about treatment meted out to them
by tribunals. From time to time complaints are received about procedure; in 1963, for example, a widow complained that proceedings
at the Ministry of Health on an appeal against the decision of a service
committee had gone on for four hours without a break, and she also
protested that she had not been permitted to deliver a statement she
had previously prepared. She had been given the impression that the
statement would have been acceptable if it had been circulated before-
hand, but 'no information was given to her that this should be done'.
The Council criticised the Ministry severely on these matters.[1] The
Council is an advisory body with no powers, but it can give publicity
to abuses, and this in itself is a useful check on ministers and tribunals.

The single most important person, as regards regulating procedure,
is the tribunal chairman, and it is here that the value of a legal training
is most felt in the tribunal world. Most lawyers, by virtue of their
training, are able to keep a firm control of the shape of proceedings,
while not allowing them to become unduly formal. A certain amount
still depends on the chairman's own firmness and authority; one chairman of a National Insurance tribunal failed to bring order to the
proceedings of his tribunal, with the result that confusion reigned
supreme at times, and the insurance officer was permitted to bully
claimants. Usually, however, lawyer chairmen are scrupulous in ensuring that both parties are able to put their cases free from interruption,
while checking lengthy irrelevancies. If the private citizen appearing
before a tribunal is not represented, the chairman will do all he can to
assist him in the presentation of his case, by questioning him to draw
out the main points of his own case, and helping him in questioning
his opponents by suggestions like, 'If I were you, I would want to ask
the witness . . .', a form of assistance which a lawyer, experienced in
the art of cross-examination, is particularly well qualified to give.
Where chairmen are not lawyers, as in the case of valuation courts, or
at public enquiries, uneducated or incoherent persons are at a far
greater disadvantage, as the chairman does far less to assist them. The
result often is that one side of the case is not clearly presented to the
tribunal, which is bound to make it more difficult for them to assess the
arguments in accordance with their true merits.

[1] Fifth Report, 1963 (H.M.S.O., 1964), paras. 63–8.

At one valuation court applications for reductions by eight house-holders were heard together, since all centred on the proximity to their homes of a centre for the training of mentally handicapped persons, an electronics factory, and the town sewage works. After the valuation officer had made his statement and one of the applicants had made a prepared statement on behalf of them all, various ratepayers began contributing information and disputing points in the valuation officer's statement with him, in a rather disorganised fashion, with the result that the court was presented with a mass of unassorted information with no clear argument in favour of the ratepayers presented; it was left to the court to bring order to this mass of fact. This rarely happens where a lawyer is in the chair.

At public enquiries, the inspector plays a passive role, doing little more than inviting each objector or his representative to speak in turn, and inviting the opposing party to comment after each speech by or on behalf of an objector. The frequent presence of lawyers representing objectors at enquiries does mean that a certain shape is given to the proceedings, as we shall see in the next chapter, but to this the inspector contributes little. He invites persons present to speak, he asks an occasional question, and that is all. Again, an unrepresented and in-coherent objector would have difficulty in presenting his case, and could expect little in the way of assistance. Only lawyer chairmen can render more even the contest between authority and the individual which is so often the basis of tribunal proceedings.

The chairman's stature and training can also affect relations between tribunals and their clerks. If the chairman is not a lawyer, the clerk is often the only person on or connected with the 'bench' who has a detailed knowledge of the law and material factors of the case under consideration. This may result in his taking an active part in the pro-ceedings, and in the members of the tribunal leaning heavily on him for advice. At one valuation court, the clerk had been a valuation officer, and had long experience both of rating law and of court proceedings, while the chairman and members were lay people. At the hearing, the clerk quite frequently questioned ratepayers, and would sometimes intervene to explain points of law not only to the ratepayers, but even to the members of the court. In interview, this clerk stressed very much his position as the lone expert among amateurs, and admitted quite freely that when the court retired he would often advise them on points of law and even tell them if he thought they were missing the point at issue; it should be said in fairness that both members of the tribunal and the clerk would retire from a case in which they might be deemed to be interested, members if the case concerned a property paying rates to an authority of which they are members, the clerk if the case concerned a person connected with him by ties of relationship or friendship.

The Ministry of Housing and Local Government, which pays the clerks, has no interest in the result of proceedings before the courts, but in view of the dangers implicit in the position of clerks in many tribunals, as mentioned earlier, it is important to remember that the presence of a chairman with the knowledge and the authority conferred by a legal training is one important means of ensuring that clerks do not come to assume the role of adviser on the complexities of law and substance in cases before tribunals.

Nonetheless, not all chairmen, whether lawyers or not, are equally good, or bad, at their job. The valuation court clerk referred to earlier said that although he himself was in a fairly powerful position, he knew of other courts where the clerk was 'a clerk with a very small "c" '. Another feature which varied widely was the amount of freedom given to parties to put their case. The two medical appeal tribunals visited were very different. At the first, the insurance officer began by stating the facts of the case in some detail, as they were presented on the papers submitted by the appellant, occasionally asking the appellant if he agreed that the facts he was presenting were correct. The appellant or his representative then made a statement in reply, and if the appellant was represented, after his representative had spoken, the appellant was invited to comment. The chairman and members would then ask any questions they had of the appellant and the insurance officer before taking the appellant for examination, if this was deemed necessary.[1] The tribunal would then deliberate and inform the appellant that he would be advised of the result shortly.

At the other tribunal the proceedings were briefer. The insurance officer confined himself to a mere statement of the facts in one or two short sentences, and appellants or their representatives were also very brief. The chairman might ask one or two questions before the examination or deliberation. Appellants were given little chance to

[1] Appellants have no right to an examination; this may be carried out at the discretion of the tribunal.

add anything to the statements they had made on their application forms. While it is true that tribunals already have a considerable amount of information before them when the hearing opens, nonetheless if the appellant is allowed to speak more freely he is more likely to feel that he has had a fair hearing; one appellant, represented by a trade union officer, said to the latter after the hearing, 'Well, we lost, but you told them!' From the point of view of inspiring public confidence in the system, it is preferable that parties be allowed to air their views reasonably freely. This happens in most cases.

Apart from their ability to ensure that proceedings take a clear and orderly shape, lawyer chairmen often explain to the parties what they must prove in order to succeed in their applications to the tribunal. In one redundancy payments case where the employee was represented by a solicitor, the chairman explained at length the definition of redundancy laid down by the Act, and explained that the employee's representative must show that dismissal had resulted from a reduction in the respondent firm's overall requirements for a particular kind of work. The applicant had been a garage forecourt attendant who had been replaced by two women who, as a witness for the respondent explained, cost the firm less in wages and were more attractive to the clientele. The chairman said that while the applicant was redundant 'in the ordinary sense of the term', these circumstances did not amount to redundancy in the sense required by the Act. The applicant's representative could not refute this, despite encouragement from the chair to 'be very bold and suggest that this was redundancy in the sense required by the Act'. The applicant lost his case. The chairman's intervention in explaining the requirements of the law saved much time.

By contrast, at one valuation court hearing, a ratepayer was allowed to expand for over half an hour on the threats and depravity of building workers on a site adjacent to the house she occupied, before the chairman explained that the court's practice was to make a temporary reduction at a standard rate of £2 if such nuisance as this was shown to be excessive. Provided a lawyer has in addition those attributes of character which enable him firmly to control the proceedings, he will be better able than a layman to see that cases are conducted with fairness, clarity and dispatch. Procedure is determined largely by chairmanship.

One other feature of tribunal proceedings which we might discuss

E

here is the way in which applicants are informed of rights of appearance before tribunals. In most cases where an appeal arises out of an official decision applicants are notified on the form advising them of the decision that they may, if they wish, appeal to the relevant tribunal. Since the Franks Report, which contains a recommendation to the effect that such notification should be automatic,[1] it has been made so in all cases considered in the present study. Statements are often exchanged by the two sides, and these are submitted to the members of the tribunal; where medical matters are involved it is sometimes deemed to be unwise to tell an applicant the truth about his own condition, which can lead to vagueness and the use of euphemisms such as 'constitutional causes' both in documents and in proceedings, so that the evidence appears vague and incomplete. This can sometimes benefit an applicant, at least financially. In one case medical reasons for the slowness of a patient's recovery from the effects of an accident were concealed and he got an extension of the duration of his industrial injury benefit, despite the Insurance Officer's suspicions, which turned out to have been justified; a month later the applicant died of cancer of the stomach.

In the field of mental health the tendency to secrecy of mental hospital authorities about their assessment both of the patient's condition and of other circumstances, such as the proposed accommodation for him, gave rise to concern ventilated through the National Council for Civil Liberties that this secrecy was unduly prejudicing the chances of applicants gaining their release through their appearances before the tribunals. All or parts of the hospital's report on the patient's condition were often concealed from both him and his representative; furthermore, it was frequently the practice to conceal the findings of the person reporting on conditions in the household where it was proposed that the patient should live if he were released. Patients and their representatives thus have no chance to question these two important documents, and the National Council for Civil Liberties made representations to the Council on Tribunals to the effect that the patient's representative should be allowed to see these reports in their entirety. If such facilities are not granted, the patient is at once at a disadvantage at the hearing, though the possibly harmful effects of giving patients access to this information must also be recognised.

[1] Cmnd 218, Recommendation 9.

In their fifth Report, the Council on Tribunals reported that they had taken these matters up with the Minister of Health, and had achieved some improvements, although they had not succeeded in removing all the causes which the National Council for Civil Liberties had found for complaint; the latter body now seems more contented about these tribunals and, believing that it is particularly important for persons appearing before these tribunals to be represented, the National Council for Civil Liberties has instituted a scheme whereby volunteers are made available to represent applicants. Apart from the fact that the representative is likely to be more coherent in presenting the case than the applicant himself, an argument which has a particular force in the field of mental health, the representative may be granted access to information which it would not be wise to disclose to patients themselves. The National Council for Civil Liberties urge their volunteers to examine the documents they are shown with care, and in particular to scrutinise any allegations of violence on behalf of their clients, and any statements of doubtful accuracy, with a view, if necessary, to bringing these in question at the hearing. On the other hand, it is still the practice for the members of the tribunal to receive a confidential report from the hospital. It has not been easy to reconcile the demands of medical prudence with those of justice.[1]

Tribunal proceedings are generally informal; the idea that appearing before a tribunal should be like 'a chat around a table' still holds considerable sway among those who operate the tribunal system. Chairmen try to reassure those appearing before them and often assist them in presenting their cases. At public enquiries, on the other hand, the inspector plays a more passive role, and the procedure is largely determined by the participants. Because legal representation is frequently resorted to at these enquiries, the procedure tends to be rather formal, since lawyers adhere rigidly to the ways they have learned in the courts. By contrast, at the Oxford Local Government Boundary Review Enquiry few lawyers were present and the procedure was informal, with a free process of questioning and discussion between objectors and the inspector.[2] A similar informality of procedure also occurs at

---

[1] Fifth Report, 1963 (H.M.S.O., 1964), Section III; National Council for Civil Liberties, *Notes for Representatives*.
[2] I am indebted to Mr Robert Baxter, now of The Queen's University of Belfast, for describing the proceedings at this enquiry to me.

minor planning enquiries where legal representation is not resorted to. At public enquiries the objectors or their representatives largely determine the procedure followed.

A number of other features of enquiry procedure have aroused concern at various times. In 1955 Professor H. W. R. Wade wrote that 'the objectors are not in a position of being able to wait for the case against them to be proved, so that they may know the arguments which they will have to rebut. They are fighting with a phantom opponent, for the initiative is put upon them and they may be in the dark as to the official motives behind the proposed order.'[1]

The Franks Committee entered a demand that before an enquiry opened, objectors should be informed of the case they would have to meet,[2] and in response the Ministry of Housing and Local Government exhorted local authorities to give objectors more information about the reasons for their decisions where these had led to a demand for an enquiry. In Circular 9/58, they said that where a local authority desired to purchase land or property compulsorily they should prepare a written statement, 'setting out clearly the reasons for its proposals', to be made available to those affected 'as early as possible' in order that 'they will be better able to present their case'.[3] They also urged the giving of more detailed and clearer reasons for refusing planning permission, in a passage quoted earlier,[4] a statement which should be further amplified if the applicant decided to appeal to the Minister, in order that he might know the full case for the authority's decision. Such increased willingness to give information would not only result in fairer enquiries; it might also reduce the number of appeals by making persons affected by decisions of these kinds more ready to accept them. That the Ministry was concerned to drive the lessons of Circular 9/58 home was evident when their Chief Housing and Planning Inspector repeated much of the advice it contained in an address to the Town Planning Institute early in 1960.[5] Under the Tribunals and Enquiries Act, the Council on Tribunals is empowered to investigate any matter relating to a public enquiry which is brought to its notice.

[1] *Public Administration*, 1955, p. 390.
[2] Cmnd 218, paras. 280–5.
[3] Paragraph 5.   [4] See p. 13 *supra*.
[5] S. G. Beaufoy, in the Town Planning Institute *Journal*, March 1960, pp. 86–9.

It was not long before the Council was asked to exercise this power. The facts of the so-called 'Chalkpit case' are too well known to require detailed description; they may be summarised as follows. In 1960 Essex County Council refused an application for planning permission to mine chalk near Saffron Walden, a decision against which the applicant company appealed, with the result that a public enquiry was held, after which the Minister reversed the county authority's decision. The proceedings of the enquiry, and the Minister's subsequent action, were the subject of complaints to the Council on Tribunals, on the grounds that the Minister had rejected his inspector's findings without giving his reasons, and that neighbouring landlords, who were in the position of 'third parties' at the enquiry, had not been given sufficient chance to comment on the way the granting of the permission would affect their interests.[1] This case was followed very shortly by another, this time involving a proposal by the state-owned steel enterprise, Richard Thomas and Baldwin, to mine iron ore near Banbury, which also gave rise to a public enquiry, about which it was complained that Richard Thomas and Baldwin had refused to divulge information requested by objectors. At the time, the Council on Tribunals were able to obtain little satisfaction with regard to either of these incidents; with regard to the Banbury case, the Lord Chancellor felt that appellants could not be compelled to disclose information; the most that could be done was to point out that such failure might be prejudicial to the success of an appeal.[2] However, in 1962 the Council were able to submit a draft set of procedural rules for public enquiries to the Government, which was accepted with few amendments.[3] The proposals are largely concerned with the presentation of ministerial decisions, but also provide that forty-two days' notice should be given of the holding of an enquiry, that local authorities should inform the other parties to the dispute of the submissions upon which they propose to rely at the enquiry, including any ministerial directives to which their representatives intend to refer. These rights were to be extended to 'third parties' to the dispute, so meeting one of the chief complaints arising from the Chalkpit case. The adoption of these

[1] Third Report, 1961 (H.M.S.O., 1962), Section IV, paras. 56–62.
[2] Third Report, Section IV, paras. 62–70.
[3] Fourth Report, paras. 23–39.

proposals by the Government has led to a greater uniformity of procedure before and during public enquiries.

A public enquiry opens with the representatives of the authority explaining their decisions or proposals, depending on the type of issue being considered, and copies of these statements are generally distributed among the other parties attending the hearing. The inspector asks questions of the authority's officers as they occur to him, and afterwards he invites the other parties to cross-examine each official in turn. Each objector or appellant then presents his case, with such witnesses as he may call, his method of proceeding being largely at his own discretion, or that of his representative, though all witnesses, including objectors or appellants themselves, are, of course, subject to cross-examination by the authority's representative, and at any point the inspector can intervene to put questions to a witness. When all the objectors have been heard, the inspector adjourns the enquiry; subsequent proceedings and the announcement of decisions will be discussed later. Enquiry proceedings can become acrimonious; at the enquiry into a proposal for the erection of a chimney referred to earlier, the representatives of each of the two firms angrily accused the other of selfishly putting their interests before those of the country, and at one point the one representative demanded of the opposing firm's managing director, who was testifying, whether there was something 'ungentlemanly and morally wrong' about his client's proposals, which were the subject of the enquiry. Inspectors play little part in guiding the proceedings, and at this particular enquiry, some stormy passages occurred without intervention from the chair, apart from occasional questions. Where the subject-matter is beyond lay comprehension, the inspector sits with assessors expert in the relevant fields; in the case just referred to he had need of assessors expert in aviation and metallurgy. Depending on the extent and bitterness of the conflict, the length of these enquiries can vary greatly; of the three attended, one lasted two-and-a-half hours, one two-and-a-half days, and the third nearly three weeks. The procedure, such as it is, is simple and flexible; it is not, however, at all helpful to the unrepresented lay person appearing, unless he happens to be a fluent speaker skilled in the art of clear exposition. Possibly for this reason, whereas at tribunals legal representation is rare, at enquiries representation of some kind appears to be almost universal, and legal representatives are frequently brought in.

Thus, between personnel and procedure there is a close relationship. Lawyer chairmen are often adept at obtaining an orderly procedure under which everyone gets a fair hearing, and which, in addition, provides assistance for the lay party to proceedings. Without such firm and orderly conduct, proceedings can easily become confused and even chaotic, and the need for representation is often more pressing, which gives rise to other problems. These are discussed in the next chapter.

IV ADVOCACY

From time to time, there has been considerable discussion as to whether persons appearing before administrative tribunals and enquiries need representatives to put their cases before the adjudicators, and, if they do, there is the question of what form it should take. It is a saying among lawyers that 'he who fights his own case has a fool for a client', yet before tribunals, legal representatives are usually rare, and parties frequently appear before them without the assistance of advocates, whether professional or otherwise.

The function of the advocate was defined by the late Lord Birkett of Ulverston as a person whose duty it is 'to devote himself completely to his task whatever he himself may think of the charges, and to lay aside every other duty, so that he may watch constantly in the interests of the accused, and say for him all that he would wish to say for himself, were he able to do so'.[1]

The citizen before court or tribunal has neither the legal knowledge nor, usually, the eloquence, to present his own case effectively, and he needs the assistance of a trained advocate to do it for him, whether in a sensational murder trial or in contesting an official's refusal to grant him an unemployment benefit, so the argument runs. In the words of the Franks Committee, 'many people are quite unable to present their own case coherently',[2] and they therefore have need of assistance. Poverty, however, is often even more of a problem than it is before the courts of law. To take what might be described as a paradigm case, before National Assistance tribunals, applicants for benefit are, 'almost by definition . . . unable to afford any expenses in connection with their appeals'.[3] If a person were applying for National Assistance because, in the words of the Act, his means were insufficient to meet his needs, his case is going to appear weak, to say the least, if it turns out that he can afford to brief a solicitor or even counsel to present his case. The solution most often proposed is that the system of legal aid should be extended to cover tribunal proceedings. Such an

[1] *Six Great Advocates* (Penguin Books, 1961), p. 100.
[2] Cmnd 218, para. 85.
[3] Pollard, *op. cit.*, p. 54.

extension was recommended by the Franks Committee[1] and more recently a legal correspondent of the weekly paper *New Society* urged the extension of legal aid to tribunals in strong terms, dismissing all the usual arguments put forward against encouraging more frequent resort to legal representatives:

> Before the Rent Officer, the Rent Tribunal, the rate assessment committee, before the Industrial Tribunal, the National Insurance Tribunal and many others, the ordinary person has to rely on his own pocket for professional representation or advice. . . . It is argued that, if professional representation were encouraged, the proceedings would become formal, take longer and become too rigid for the tribunals to function efficiently; and these arguments are in part true. But the tribunals have now become part of the administration of justice, and justice must be seen to be done: public justice has always demanded a certain element of formality and predictability of procedure, coupled with demonstrably fair opportunity for every party to put his case fully before the tribunal. Without professional representation those standards cannot be consistently attained. The failure of successive governments to extend legal aid to tribunal proceedings is wholly indefensible.[2]

Such is the argument in favour of extending legal aid, and, indeed, for legal representation in general. Only a trained lawyer can present the citizen's case properly; only if the state gives financial assistance can citizens be assured of this necessary assistance.

One must remember, though, that before some tribunals the role of the representative, however able, may in the nature of things be restricted. In some cases a person's character or sincerity may be at issue, as was the case with conscientious objector tribunals, where the criterion for granting registration as a conscientious objector was the sincerity or otherwise of the appellant's pacifist views. Sincerity cannot be represented; Robert Pollard, wrote that 'the applicant is not required actually to attend himself, but since it is his conscience which is under examination, he generally finds it advisable to do so'.[3] Similarly in medical cases, such as industrial injury cases coming before medical

---

[1] Cmnd 218, para. 89, and Recommendation 16.
[2] *New Society*, 19 January 1967, pp. 87–8.
[3] *Op. cit.*, p. 3.

boards or medical appeal tribunals, the applicant must himself be present for examination and diagnosis by the medical members of the tribunal. The part the representative can play is restricted in the very nature of the case. Pains cannot be examined vicariously.

Before the appearance of the Franks Report, legal representation was not permitted before several tribunals. The Committee recommended that this prohibition should be relaxed,[1] and in almost all cases this has now been done. Before most tribunals legal representation is still rare, partly, no doubt, because no legal aid is available. Of the tribunals investigated, only before industrial tribunals was the employment of lawyers at all common. In this case the issues are often highly complex, the amounts involved may be comparatively large; a redundancy payment case may involve several hundred pounds, and the proceedings tend to be long and difficult for the layman to follow. Before these tribunals, therefore, some 50 per cent of persons appearing bring solicitors or counsel. Otherwise it is rare; in the case of one rent assessment committee, out of eighty-eight cases heard to date, only seven landlords and four tenants have brought lawyers. Before Rent Tribunals perhaps one in five cases sees the appearance of a lawyer on one side or the other, while lawyers only very occasionally appear before such bodies as medical appeal tribunals and National Insurance appeal tribunals. It is, perhaps, as well to point out that the volume of tribunal work is such that if demands for legal representation became at all common the legal profession would soon be unable to cope with the extra demands made upon them; this becomes evident from the work load of tribunals as described in Chapter II.

There are further points that one must make about legal representation before tribunals. Many tribunal chairmen, even when they are themselves lawyers, regard the appearance of lawyers at their tribunals with some apprehension. In the words of one chairman, they are often 'advocates of the obvious'. The difficulty arises from the fact that a lawyer will invariably adhere to the letter of court procedure. Lawyers believe that this procedure alone will secure fairness, and its use also gives them what might almost be described as a sense of security. One solicitor admitted that he much preferred appearing in court to appearing in tribunal proceedings; the latter were far less predictable. In an important respect, however, the usual method of presenting evidence

1 Cmnd 218, paras. 83–8, and Recommendation 15.

in court is inappropriate to tribunals. In court, the case is often heard *de novo*, especially in criminal proceedings; having taken the oath, witnesses are first asked their names and addresses, and give their evidence starting from the most basic points, in response to counsel's questioning, beginning with such items as whether they were at a certain place at a certain time, and whether they saw certain persons or the occurrence of certain events.

In the case of tribunals much of the basic factual evidence will already be before the members in the form of written statements previously made by the parties. Ratepayers appealing against their assessments make a proposal that it be reduced, giving their reasons. Claimants of national insurance, industrial injury, and other benefits have, previously to the hearing, completed a claim form, on the basis of which an officer has already made a decision, usually given in a written statement available to the tribunal, and the applicant will have completed a further statement of his reasons for appealing against the official's decision. All these documents are duplicated and are usually circulated to the chairman and members of the tribunal in advance; in addition, it is often the practice for the insurance officer concerned to submit comments on the appeal. Hence, before the hearing opens, the members of the adjudicating body already have before them a considerable amount of information about the circumstances of the case; lawyers appearing on behalf of claimants, however, almost always insist on going through it all again in open court, needlessly prolonging the hearing and wearying the tribunal. This method of proceeding is all the more inappropriate in view of the fact, mentioned in the previous chapter, that even where tribunals are empowered to administer the oath, they rarely do so. Thus there is little need to have evidence given in all its detail, since it is seldom given with the help of God or under the threat of perjury proceedings; usually evidence given at the hearing is given no guarantee of accuracy which is not given in the case of the written submission previously made. The examination-in-chief procedure is retained by lawyers chiefly from force of habit.

The system of question and answer also prolongs hearings unnecessarily. The need felt by lawyers to begin at the beginning and work through to the end, presenting a coherent case in the form of witnesses' answers to questions, is time-consuming, and often a written or verbal *ex parte* statement would serve the purpose equally well, and in much

less time. Objectors at public enquiries, for example, may be examined
at length on matters of fact which could have been presented more
briefly in prepared statements, as is the normal practice of local
authority officials appearing before these enquiries. Take the following
extract from a solicitor's examination of his client at an enquiry into
objections to proposed new parking restrictions:

> *Representative* (a solicitor): Your name is John Smith?
> *Witness:* Yes.
> *Solicitor:* You are the owner of the Restaurant Supreme and the
> Excelsior hairdressing salon, are you not?
> *Witness:* I am.
> *Solicitor:* And is it your belief that the enforcement of these restric-
> tions would seriously affect your trade?
> *Witness:* That is my view.
> *Solicitor:* Is it the case that 90 per cent of your daytime trade comes
> in by car, and would have to park an appreciable distance away from
> your premises under the proposed restrictions?
> *Witness:* Yes, they would, and they would have to cross a bridge
> exposed to wind and rain on foot to reach my businesses.[1]

The material so presented could have been more compactly presented
in a prepared statement, and time would have been saved. Public
enquiries sometimes become endurance tests of some severity for all
concerned; the one in question lasted nearly three days, while another
attended by the present author went on for three weeks. It was the
over-formal and dilatory procedure adopted at public enquiries by
lawyers that caused Denys Munby to write some years ago urging a
change of practice:

> It should be perfectly possible to adopt a reasonable procedure which
> allows for full discussion of all the issues, critical examination of
> the case put up by the public body in question, elucidation of new
> facts and the presentation of relevant evidence and argument, with-
> out the full legal procedure of the law courts in the matter of the
> hearing of 'witnesses', formal rules of evidence, and formal cross-
> examination, and without turning a public enquiry into a forum for
> the display of counsel's eloquence.

That last phrase raises one additional point; lawyers often feel that they

[1] Names fictitious.

must be seen by their clients to earn their fees. Mr Munby went on to conclude that a simpler, more informal and flexible procedure should be worked out by civil servants and the legal profession, and said that if this were not done, 'it is to be feared that the question recently raised, "Are Public Enquiries a Farce?" will have to be answered, "Yes, because the lawyers have made them so." '[1] The same danger might threaten tribunals, if legal representation were to become common before them.[2]

Nonetheless, as we remarked in the last chapter, without representation tribunal proceedings do tend to become something of a battle between David and Goliath. On the one hand, the official presenting the departmental case is likely to be more highly educated than the average citizen appearing before the tribunal; he is also likely to have gained considerable experience in the presentation of cases to tribunals. Insurance officers, valuation officers, and their like, have to appear frequently before the tribunals relevant to the fields in which they work, as part of their duties, and apart from the experience they acquire, they may become acquainted with the foibles and scruples of chairmen or members of the tribunals in their areas. Facing these officials is usually a member of the public, often nervous, perhaps poorly educated, and almost certainly completely lacking experience of the art of advocacy before court or tribunal. It is only where the duty of the tribunal is to arbitrate between private individuals, as in the case of rent tribunals, rent assessment committees, or agricultural land tribunals, or between an individual and a private company, as where an industrial tribunal hears a claim for a redundancy payment, that some sort of rough equality is likely to exist between the parties, assuming, of course, that neither side engages a representative. It is here, in bringing greater equality to the contest, that, as we saw in the last chapter, the lawyer plays his most important role, and this he does from the chair. A lawyer in the chair of a tribunal is no less conscious than his colleague appearing before him on occasions, of the demands fairness makes on procedure; his training will see to that. But he is better able to further this cause from the chair than he is in the position of advocate, without causing undue prolongation of the proceedings.

[1] *Public Administration*, 1956, p. 184.
[2] Tribunal Claimers now appear to have persuaded the Council on Tribunals that legal representation is neither necessary nor desirable. Report for 1967 (H.M.S.O., 1968), paras. 58–61.

It is in taking tribunal chairs that lawyers make their most effective contribution to administrative justice.

A second problem confronting the advocate before administrative tribunals and enquiries is the need for expertise. The fields with which these bodies concern themselves often require specialist knowledge in those charged with making decisions, and no less from those appearing before them. Agricultural land tribunals, for instance, often have to consider cases in which the decision hinges on the merits or otherwise of farming techniques, or on those of particular types of farming; hence their members other than the chairman are required to be knowledge-able in the field of agriculture. However, it may well be that the advocate appearing before these tribunals also needs to be an expert, which lawyers seldom, if ever, are; their lack of knowledge may seriously hamper them in cross-examination; for example, they will often be unable to expose the technical weaknesses of an opponent's case: this can only be done through questioning from members of the tribunal themselves.

If the effectiveness of advocacy is not reduced, nonetheless the major points may be entirely missed, and also, even where advocacy is brilliant, it may be useless without authoritative backing. Before medical appeal tribunals, one cannot normally hope to win a case without an independent surgeon's or specialist's report casting doubt on the contentions of the insurance officer and the medical board. One cannot expect the tribunal, with its specialist members, to take notice of the beliefs of an appellant or of his lay representative. An appellant may sincerely and honestly believe that some enduring pain or disability was caused by an industrial accident, because it either made itself apparent or became more pronounced, shortly after the accident in question, even though in fact the cause may be quite different. Before medical appeal tribunals, such cases are quite common, and the tribunals do not accept the Humean view of causation; in support of advocacy, however brilliant, they require the authority of expert evidence that there is indeed a causal connection between the pain or disability and the precedent accident or injury. At their dis-cretion they may seek such evidence for themselves by examining the appellant at the hearing, though they are not required to do so, but here again, the resultant depends on expert assessment of the evidence, and not on advocacy.

Thirdly, it must be said that the law involved in tribunal proceedings is quite frequently outside the main stream, so to speak, of legal practice. As we saw earlier, legal representation is not common, and hence solicitors do not easily or quickly acquire a body of experience in tribunal advocacy, another reason, perhaps, for their adherence to court practice; they know no other. But tribunals are frequently concerned with interpreting statutes which are seldom the subject of litigation in 'other places'; lawyers thus have little incentive to master the intricacies of, say, the Redundancy Payments Act of 1965, the National Insurance Acts, the Agriculture Acts of 1947 and 1958, or the National Assistance Act of 1949, to name but a few statutes providing for the setting up of tribunals. Furthermore, tribunals sometimes have their own body of case law. In some cases, the appeal lies to a court of law, usually the High Court, at least on points of law, though from the General Commissioners of Inland Revenue, appeals on both law and substance lie to the Chancery Division. The Franks Committee recommended that appeal to the courts on points of law should be extended to cover all tribunals where there was no other right of appeal,[1] but this has not always been done. Where it has, the appeal cases and decisions are, of course, reported in the way that other court cases are, and these reports are readily available to lawyers. In several cases, however, appeal lies not to a court but to a superior tribunal, whose announcement of decisions may vary in form considerably in a way which is important from the point of view of the advocate. On the one hand, appeal from decisions of valuation courts is to the Lands Tribunal, a prestigious and formal body whose cases are reported and published in the same way as those of the courts. In the social security field, however, appeals lie to commissioners whose decisions are circulated by the Ministry to tribunal chairmen and Ministry officers, but are not part of the regular Law Reports and are released in periodic publications by the Stationery Office. Not only are these decisions harder for the citizen to obtain; they are also so voluminous that to keep abreast of them would be a heavy task; between 1959 and 1963, the National Insurance Commissioner and his deputies heard over 2,000 cases a year.[2] Unless an advocate were to specialise in appearing

---

[1] Cmnd 218, para. 107 and Recommendation 27.
[2] Reports of the Ministry of Pensions and National Insurance, 1959–63 (H.M.S.O., 1960–64, *seriatim*).

before tribunals, which none do, since as things are at present, the volume of work is not sufficient to justify such specialisation, he is not likely to become familiar with the body of case law built up by tribunals and appellate bodies, or often, indeed, with the statutes themselves. Hence one finds that the phenomenon of tribunal chairmen having to explain the law to lawyers appearing before them is not uncommon. Chairmen of agricultural land tribunals frequently have to remind persons appearing before them, including lawyers, of the discretion given to these tribunals in Notice to Quit cases to decide the issue on the basis of the 'Proviso', that the landlord's proposed action must appear to be fair and reasonable.[1] At a hearing attended by the present author, the chairman read out the 'Proviso' and asked the tenant's solicitor if he wished the tribunal to apply it. Again, at an industrial tribunal, in a case where both parties were legally represented, the chairman had to intervene to explain the definition of redundancy contained in the Act, since the solicitors appeared not to have understood it.[2] The applicant lost his case, but had he and his representative been more familiar with the requirements of the Act, and with an appeal case in which this matter had been the subject of a High Court ruling, they would probably never have brought the case to the tribunal. This situation may be improved by the publication of Neville Vandyk's guide to the functions of the various tribunals, which presents many facts to the legal profession and the public which were not easily available before, thus easing the passage of a solicitor or counsel asked to appear on behalf of a client in tribunal proceedings,[3] but the legal profession has not yet entirely come to terms with the needs of administrative justice.

In certain cases other professional men may be as good or even better advocates before tribunals than lawyers, by virtue of their expert knowledge both of substance and of the relevant law. Thus chartered accountants often appear on behalf of their clients before the General and Special Commissioners of Income Tax, while chartered valuers may perform the same service before valuation courts or rent tribunals, and agricultural valuers before agricultural land tribunals. At this point, interest groups once more become involved. Some pay particular

---

[1] See p. 32 above.   [2] See p. 53 above for an account of this case.
[3] Neville D. Vandyk, Solicitor of the Supreme Court, *Tribunals and Enquiries* (Oyez Publications, London, 1965).

solicitors or other professional men retainers to secure for their members the services of a professional advocate or representative, and incidentally offer some inducement to the persons so retained to specialise in work before tribunals in the field concerned, and so to acquire both knowledge and experience. The National Farmers' Union, for example, have several solicitors on retainers, and one tribunal officer went so far as to say that if tenants threatened with eviction had any sense, they would ask the N.F.U. to supply their representatives for the agricultural land tribunal proceedings. In other cases, especially where the resources of the clients are unlikely to be sufficient to pay solicitors' fees, interest groups sometimes endeavour to supply representatives either from among their own staffs, or by seeking volunteers from among their members. The most important instance of this is the provision by trade unions of representatives for their members; otherwise there is the National Council for Civil Liberties' effort to provide representatives from among its members for mental hospital patients applying for their release to mental health appeal tribunals.

Persons appearing before these last tribunals are often, almost by definition, more in need of representatives than most; they may be vague, incoherent, or simply unable to comprehend the facts alleged about them by the hospital authorities. The importance of representation in terms of success in procuring the release of patients is shown by the following figures; between November 1960 and December 1963, 21 per cent of applicants represented secured their release, as compared with only 11 per cent of those not represented. Representation is important not only because the patient may be unable effectively to present his own case, but also because the representative can often see material which would not be shown to the patient himself. But above all, it is the element of chance introduced by the varying character, background and even personal appearance of applicants which needs to be reduced; the present writer was told of one applicant for release who was a highly educated technical man, intelligent and coherent, who, though unrepresented, procured his release; the tribunal member who described this case said that 'very probably, the answer would have been very different for a less well-educated man'. Very often mental patients and their relatives cannot afford professional representation.

Quite early in their existence, mental health review tribunals

F

attracted the attention of the National Council for Civil Liberties,[1] who received a number of complaints about their working, and on 19 December 1962 representatives of the National Council met the Council on Tribunals to discuss mental health tribunals. The NCCL had found that it was in cases where the patient was seriously deranged or otherwise deficient or mentally ill, that injustices were most likely to arise. They complained of the frequency with which the tribunals did not give the reasons for their decisions, of which more later, and also complained that applicants, their relatives and their representatives were often denied information vital to the effective presentation of their case; at the meeting, the NCCL representatives 'gave instances where inadequate or misleading information had been given', and urged that representatives should be given more complete information. As a result of these representations, the Council on Tribunals recommended that the hospital authorities should make the hospital and 'home circumstances' reports available to representatives, that if the applicant were not represented he should at least be allowed to see the latter document, and, since representation was of such great importance, and became more so where the hospital authorities refused to divulge information to the patient himself but would disclose it to a representative, representation should be more easily available to applicants.

The National Council for Civil Liberties, believing that many patients did not know where they could obtain such assistance, urged the creation of panels of representatives attached to each tribunal, and later instituted a scheme whereby it would recruit volunteers to represent applicants appearing before mental health review tribunals.[2] Since then, NCCL volunteers have represented seventy-six applicants, up to November 1966, of whom thirty-one were discharged from hospital; an excellent rate of success. The volunteers are issued with detailed instructions on how to conduct the applicant's case, and are urged particularly to investigate allegations of violence made by the hospital authorities against applicants; the *Notes for Representatives* issued by NCCL state that 'On more than one occasion, we have been able to

[1] I am indebted to the National Council for Civil Liberties for information relating to mental health review tribunals.
[2] See Section III of the Fifth Report of the Council on Tribunals, 1963 (H.M.S.O., 1964).

correct inaccuracies in the hospital report and to have these deleted from the record.' But though excellent, the work of NCCL covers only a small proportion of the cases heard; there are some 800 tribunal cases a year, so that seventy-six applicants helped in four years is not many compared with the total; less than 10 per cent of the other applicants are legally represented.

Some members of these tribunals seem a little hostile to the volunteer representatives; one solicitor who sits on a mental health review tribunal said that the lay representatives tend to over-dramatise their part in the proceedings; they tended to see themselves as 'an aspiring Perry Mason' who could 'create an appalling muddle'. On the other hand, lawyers are expensive and no better able to understand the medical issues involved than the educated layman, and there is a continuing need to watch over the interests of mental patients. In 1964 the Council on Tribunals received a complaint that an applicant to a mental health review tribunal had been denied access to information which was held by the hospital authorities to give the lie to the basis of his claim for release; the Council felt that this action 'appeared almost certain to make a person in the applicant's position feel that he was being unfairly treated'.[1] No improvement in the situation was secured, but the Council felt that the question of assistance for applicants appearing before these tribunals should be further investigated. Despite the efforts of the National Council for Civil Liberties, it is all too possible still for injustices to occur in the field of mental health. The NCCL is concerned at the small number of patients it is able to help, and proposes to seek more funds and volunteers,[2] while in their Eighth Report, the Council on Tribunals have made proposals for a more comprehensive provision of representatives for mental patients.[3]

The other interest groups which provide representatives for citizens appearing before tribunals are the trade unions, whose officers undertake the presentation of members' cases before social security tribunals and in redundancy payments cases before industrial tribunals. This work is normally undertaken by a union's district or area organiser or one of his staff; sometimes there will be a legal adviser appointed

[1] Sixth Report, 1964 (H.M.S.O., 1965), para. 41.
[2] *Civil Liberty* (published by NCCL annually), 1967.
[3] Eighth Report, 1966 (H.M.S.O., 1967), para. 52.

to the area or regional office, who will undertake representation of members before tribunals. These officers generally receive little or no training for this particular task, and those interviewed said that they relied almost entirely on their experience; they had learned the job as they went along. A certain amount of training is given in the courses a full-time union officer goes through at various stages in his career, and since 1956 the Trades Union Congress Training College has provided a week-long course in Social Security which deals, among other matters, with tribunal work, both for men who may be called upon to represent their members at hearings and because on many of the tribunals concerned with social security or industrial matters, there must be a workpeople's representative, who is always a union officer, as we saw in Chapter III. This training has been somewhat extended in 1967–68 by the institution of a course for full-time officers to provide an opportunity for officers who assist members in presenting claims for benefits to local appeal tribunals and/or who serve on local advisory committees, to acquire a more thorough understanding of the social security system'.[1] Apart from this, there are a number of shorter classes or schools. Gradually, more training is being provided for union officers in this matter, but for many experience is still the only training they have received.

These men have the advantage of not being bound by the traditions of the Courts. In general, they present their cases more briefly and with less formality, and their methods are thus better adapted to tribunal proceedings. They are more ready than lawyers to recognise that the members of the tribunal already have a considerable volume of information before them, of which the representative too normally possesses copies, and that their task is to add something to this body of information if they can. They usually take care to study appeal decisions which may bind the tribunal, such as those of the National Insurance Commissioner. In the documents sent out before the hearings, containing the submissions of the two parties, it is normal practice for the insurance officer to specify any appeal cases which he proposes to cite in support of his case, and the union officer will be able to examine them for the possibility of interpreting them in his client's favour. One chairman of a National Insurance local tribunal said that trade union representatives compared very favourably with

[1] The T.U.C. Training College Prospectus for 1967–68, page 16.

lawyers when they appeared before his tribunal; he said that the union men were familiar with the procedure, and cases proceeded more quickly than they did if lawyers were present, or even than they did if the applicant were unrepresented, in which case the process of assisting him to present his case might take some time. On the other hand, it is not unknown for the untrained union officers to make mistakes. One insurance officer, experienced in proceedings before medical appeal tribunals said that before these bodies the appellant was often better off if he was not represented at all, since in such cases the chairman would conduct his case for him, whereas if the appellant were represented, and the representative made a mistake, or simply presented the case badly, the tribunal 'can do nothing more than give the appellant a chance to comment in the hope that he will grind his representative underfoot'.

In one case, a union officer represented a docker who had injured himself lifting cartons, an injury which the original medical board had predicted would pass in time; the board had therefore only made a temporary award of industrial injury benefit. Pain and weakness had persisted, however, and the claimant was now appealing against the decision on the ground that he was still disabled and a further period of grant should be allowed. During his presentation of the appellant's case, the trade union officer referred to a haemorrhage which had caused considerable trouble to the appellant. The chairman asked whether this condition had resulted from the accident, whereupon the representative replied that he did not know; he was not a medical man. This was a serious mistake; either the union should have obtained an independent consultant's opinion on the origins of the haemorrhage, or they should have refrained from mentioning it; as it was, it was a dangerous red herring. In the event, the medical members held that there was no causal relationship between the accident and the haemorrhage, and the appellant lost his case.

Trade union representatives are much less inclined to verbosity than lawyers, but they are just as liable to make mistakes; they are not specialists in tribunal proceedings any more than are lawyers; to represent a member at a tribunal is but one of the various tasks a trade union officer may be called upon to undertake, indeed, it is outside his main role as an industrial negotiator. His other tasks may range from pressing a wage claim on a reluctant employer to seeking to gain control over unofficial strikers. He cannot therefore be expected to be expert in the law and practice of tribunals.

Finally, we must consider the attitudes of Government or local authority representatives at tribunals towards the tribunal and their opponents. Usually, they do not assume the role of prosecuting counsel; they are not concerned to win their cases at all costs. As one insurance officer put it, the Minister and his representatives are concerned to be fair to claimants, and were not concerned above all with the protection of the Insurance Fund's resources. Ministry representatives do not, as a rule, seek to secure the dismissal of cases on technical points, and will not usually try to prevent the tribunal proceeding with a hearing where this could be done through some omission or irrelevancy on the part of the claimant. In one medical appeal tribunal case, an appellant presented what he claimed was fresh evidence in his case, which turned out not to be fresh evidence at all, but merely a further opinion arrived at on the basis of the facts previously known and considered at an earlier hearing of the case. On this basis, the case could have been dismissed without further ado, but the insurance officer took it upon himself to urge the tribunal not to do so, saying that the case should be considered on the merits, arguing that 'the Minister, and you yourself, Sir,[1] would not want to be unduly pernickety'. The case was heard in full, and the claim turned out to have no substance, though the appellant could not know this; he had suffered from severe tuberculosis, a fact which had been concealed from him. It was a pitiful case, but the demands of justice and sympathy did not coincide.

Similarly, valuation officers appearing before valuation courts give objective statements of the facts and the reasons for their making the assessment in dispute, and will answer any question put to them by the ratepayers. In this case a tribunal hearing is the last stage of a period of negotiations; often both parties make concessions which result in their agreeing, only leaving the agreed figure to be formally approved by the court. Thus twenty or thirty cases may be listed for hearing on a particular day, yet only three, two, one or even none at all come to court for settlement. The valuation officer will state his conclusions, describe the preceding discussions he has had with the householder, and answer any questions from his opponent or from the members of the panel. He does not obstinately or passionately defend his decision.

[1] i.e. the Chairman.

In the case of National Insurance local tribunals the position is sometimes rather different. As with other tribunals, insurance officers plead their own cases, but in these cases they are, on occasions, definitely aggressive; one officer, a red-headed lady, persistently interrupted not only the applicants for benefit, but even the chairman of the tribunal, to argue her case further. The chairman was partly to blame for not stopping her, but nonetheless, it was very noticeable that before this particular tribunal, the insurance officers were, in general, aggressive in presenting and defending their cases, and, when cases were heard in the absence of the claimant, insurance officers adopted a patronising attitude which could militate against the interests of justice; for example, a driver who had lost his licence and hence his job had appealed against refusal of unemployment benefit. The insurance officer admitted quite openly that were he to appeal to the Commissioner, the applicant would probably be granted benefit, but since the disqualification was for a period of six months, the offence which had led to it had clearly been serious. The implication was obvious, and was accepted by the tribunal, who upheld the decision to refuse benefit in the face of Commissioner's decisions which indicated that it should have been granted. In another case, the insurance officer deliberately created in the minds of the tribunal members an impression that the applicant was incurably lazy, with adverse results for his appeal. The moral for claimants is that if one wishes to be sure of justice, one should always attend the tribunal hearing. Usually, however, official representatives seek to be fair rather than to win as many cases as possible. One other danger which is sometimes apparent is that officials and tribunal members develop a close relationship which may be detrimental to applicants' chances, and which, in any case, looks suspicious to the citizen appearing at a hearing; to see one's opponent having a friendly chat with the adjudicators cannot be expected to inspire confidence in the tribunal's impartiality.[1]

The value of representation before tribunals is, perhaps, open to doubt. Lawyers have an undesirable effect on procedure, a fact particularly apparent at public enquiries, and the fact that no body of representatives, either lawyers or laymen, exists which specialises in

---

[1] The Council on Tribunals received a complaint about fraternisation between a Valuation Officer and a Valuation Court in 1967. (1967 Report (H.M.S.O., 1968), para. 89.)

tribunal work, means that representatives can either prolong the proceedings uselessly or make mistakes which may be fatal to their clients' case. It would seem, in short, that he who fights his own case in the field of administrative justice may not always have a fool for a client, particularly since most chairmen are generous with help for unrepresented, unschooled citizens appearing before them.

Where tribunals are called upon to arbitrate between citizen and citizen, as in the case of rent tribunals or agricultural land tribunals, rather than between authority and the individual, the problems are rather different. The element of inequality produced by the experience officials have the chance to gain, as compared with the citizen's lack of it, does not arise. However, one major problem for the chairman may be keeping the peace between the parties. This is sometimes a serious problem for rent tribunals, where chairmen need to be very firm indeed. In one case, a landlord assessed the value of his tenant's furniture at a far higher figure than the tenant thought reasonable, and he tried to intervene to dispute the figure, whereupon the chairman told him that since the landlord had not interrupted him, he must extend the same courtesy in return. In such cases, the presence of representatives may help to keep the temperature down, as it were, though if one side only is represented this can create inequality. One agricultural land tribunal clerk invariably informed the other party if he heard that one party was briefing solicitor, counsel, or any other kind of representative, otherwise the represented party might gain an advantage which the tribunal would have to seek to remove.

Another somewhat similar problem is that of parties who, either by design or default, fail to appear at the tribunal hearing. In order to prevent obstruction and to save time, most tribunals are empowered to proceed in the absence of one party,[1] and, as we saw in the case of National Insurance local tribunals, not to appear may be to expose yourself to injustice. Where a tribunal's duty is to arbitrate between citizens, the absence of one party may make it almost impossible for the tribunal to obtain a balanced picture of the circumstances. A landlord applying to the rent tribunal for permission to evict a tenant protected because the rent had been fixed by the tribunal during the preceding six months,[2] on the ground that the tenant was in arrears

---

[1] This is not the case with industrial tribunals.

[2] The period of security of tenure guaranteed to a tenant after a rent tribunal hearing is six months under the Furnished Lettings Act of 1946.

to the extent of some £75, found himself without an opponent at the hearing. Because the tenant did not appear, the tribunal was unable to ask him to explain why he had not paid his rent, and hence they could not discover whether there were any extenuating circumstances which they ought to take into consideration. The tribunal had perforce to agree to reduce the period of security, but felt that the position was unsatisfactory in view of the absence of the tenant; nothing was known of his circumstances. If both parties appear, a more thorough examination of all the circumstances of the case is possible; at a rent assessment committee with both parties present, every fact about the flat involved was exhaustively discussed, as were rents of other flats in the same building, their size in comparison to the letting in question, the exact position of damp patches, the amenities of the area, the number of toilets and relations between the various tenants. Rent tribunals are often equally thorough, but this is only possible if both parties are present and able to give the necessary information.

As with other tribunals, inequalities of ability between the parties must be corrected by the chairman. Often, absentee landlords are represented by house agents or surveyors who thus acquire experience of the rent tribunals and rent assessment committees in their areas, or one party may brief a solicitor or counsel, as we mentioned earlier. In such cases the chairman must help the weaker party if a balanced picture is to be presented on which the tribunal may ground its decision. At one rent tribunal a landlady was accompanied by a solicitor, and the chairman questioned the tenant extensively on the alleged facts, such as the extent and cost of repairs undertaken by him which were properly the landlady's responsibility, the condition of the property and the efficiency of the common services provided, whereas the landlady's solicitor was left to his own devices. The extent of such inequality varies widely; some individuals are fluent and persuasive; others barely coherent.

Thus there are many shortcomings in present provisions for advocacy in administrative justice, and with them come dangers of unintended injustice. The tribunals themselves are often able to overcome these problems, and acquire considerable skill in doing so. We can repeat the conclusion reached in the previous chapter that this is the lawyer's most important contribution to securing that administrative tribunals are just in their treatment of those who come before them.

V DECISION-MAKING AND THE DISPENSING OF JUSTICE

All tribunals are arbitratory bodies. In some respects, as we have seen in earlier chapters, there are large differences between those tribunals whose task it is to arbitrate between authority and the individual and those whose duty it is to reconcile disputes between citizen and citizen. This difference may, for example, affect procedure; chairmen of the latter type of tribunal need to keep a firm control over the proceedings, otherwise there is a danger that the hearing will degenerate into an angry quarrel between the parties; equally, where one party is a government department, the chairman has the task of ensuring that both sides are able to place their cases fairly before the tribunal. But for the purpose of the present chapter, we may ignore this particular distinction. In the matter of decisions all tribunals are similar and akin to the courts of law, especially where the latter are concerned with civil proceedings; they have to decide which of the parties is in the right, and what benefit should accrue to the winner. Like the courts, all tribunals have a degree of discretion, though this varies widely in scope from tribunal to tribunal. Some merely make an affirmative or negative decision; unemployment assistance, for example, is paid at a fixed weekly rate and once the tribunal has decided to make an award, its task is over. Other tribunals have to assess the value of such things as disabilities, nuisances or defects from the point of view of deciding how much compensation should be paid. Medical boards and medical appeal tribunals have to decide whether a disability or pain complained of resulted from an industrial accident, and if it did, what degree of disability in terms of a percentage scale, has accrued to the applicant as a result. The loss of one eye is assessed as a 30 per cent disablement, while the amputation of a leg at the thigh is considered to be an 80 per cent disability. The percentage appropriate is determined by the boards subject to appeal to a medical appeal tribunal. Valuation courts, rent tribunals and rent assessment committees have a very wide discretion indeed, as we saw in Chapter II.

Public enquiries, however, are not adjudicatory bodies at all, at least in theory. The inspector's task is simply to collect information upon which the Minister will take his decision; this means that the decision-making procedure is completely different from that of tribunals and raises problems of its own. In this chapter, we therefore revert to the distinction between tribunals and enquiries and discuss each separately.

Before we discuss the actual working of the system it might be useful to consider briefly the concept of justice and what it is that we expect from our judges, whether in court or tribunal, when we demand that they act justly. Some philosophers have stressed the element of equity, or fairness, in justice. Decisions, if they are to be just, should be consistent with one another. Professor Perelman has written that to everyone justice suggests some kind of equality; whether it be equality in terms of merit, rank, race, works or creed, among persons possessing the same relevant characteristics (in the view of the person or body scrutinising the machinery of justice in a given society) equality must prevail: 'He who requires merit to be taken into account wants the *same* treatment for persons having equal merits. A second wants equal treatment for persons of the same needs. A third will demand just, that is, equal treatment for persons of the same social rank, and so on.' Thus justice is 'a principle of action in accordance with which beings of one and the same essential category must be treated in the same way'.[1] Other philosophers have concentrated on the notion of desert. The advocates of retribution have always contented that punishment should be in some sense equal and opposite to the crime it requites; the late Professor Bradley wrote that 'Punishment is punishment, only where it is deserved. We pay the penalty because we owe it, and for no other reason; and if punishment is inflicted for any other reason whatever than because it is merited by wrong, it is a gross immorality, *a crying injustice*, an abominable crime, and not what it pretends to be.'[2]

A. R. Manser, examining the well-worn phrase 'It serves you right', concluded that justice consists in administering to the wrongdoer an amount of retribution which is recognised as appropriate to his crime. Hence justice demands not only consistency, but also a correct assessment of what an action, disability or service is worth, and this applies

---

[1] G. Perelman, 'Concerning Justice', chapter 1 of his *The Idea of Justice and the Problem of Argument*, trans. Petrie (Routledge & Kegan Paul, 1963).
[2] Quoted in A. R. Manser, 'It Serves you Right', *Philosophy*, Oct. 1962 (my italics).

as much to assessing the rent for a shabby flat as it does to determining the length of a prison sentence appropriate to a conviction for causing grievous bodily harm.

A third demand made of judges is that their decisions should be of value to the society or to the individual; that justice should be utilitarian. The court or tribunal must arrive at the *best* solution, that is, the one which produces the greatest increase in happiness or decrease in pain; in the words of J. S. Mill, justice acts only in 'the direction conformable to the general good'.[1] Lastly, decisions must be in accordance with the law. It is no part of a tribunal's task to comment on the laws it is called upon to enforce; its decision must be in conformity with the rules drawn up and assessed in another place, the legislature.

The classic method of ensuring consistency in judicial decisions; of ensuring that 'like cases are treated alike', is the application of the doctrine of *stare decisis*. By following precedent, the judiciary ensure first that like cases are treated alike, and secondly that the law is predictable; anyone looking up the relevant precedent cases can discover what the courts will probably decide in present or future ones. In Louisiana, U.S.A., it was argued in the state supreme court that predictability was something the citizen could reasonably demand of his judges. 'The attorneys of this state have a right to rely on the rulings of this court and to expect some constancy in them where valuable property rights are affected.'[2] In addition, the obligation to follow precedent is a protection for the citizen from the possibility of judgments coloured by the personal whims and prejudices of judges.

In Britain, however, as we saw earlier,[3] administrative decisions must not be made on grounds of precedent or general rule. The courts have laid down that such decisions must be taken on the merits of the particular case in question; this principle has been applied both to licensing justices and to tribunals. The actual practice of tribunals in the matter of precedent varies considerably. In most cases there exists what was described to the present author as 'a vast submerged body of precedent'. Tribunals are likely to consider previous cases similar to that in hand and will sometimes declare that their custom is to pursue a certain line of action in all cases of a particular kind. Thus at one valuation

---

[1] *Utilitarianism*, ch. 5.
[2] Lee *v.* Jones, Louisiana, U.S.A. 1953.
[3] See pp. 7–10 above.

court hearing a case in which a ratepayer was asking for a temporary reduction in his assessment because of nuisance caused by building operations on adjacent sites, the chairman explained that in such cases the court's practice was to reduce the assessment by £2 for a period of six months, if it had been shown that the nuisance was excessive.

Some tribunals have to a degree formalised their reference to their own precedents; an Agricultural Land Tribunal clerk disclosed that he kept a register of the tribunal's previous decisions which the chairman would consult if he wished to do so. Sometimes the clerk would draw the chairman's attention to precedent cases that seemed to him to be relevant. Where there is a further appeal, to a central body or to the courts, the decisions of the superior body are usually considered to set precedents binding upon the tribunals, as we saw in the case of medical appeal tribunals, where the commissioner has determined, among other things, that certain procedural rules shall be observed.[1] Courts or superior tribunals also clarify the law and lay down binding ruling for the lower bodies to follow, of course. Thus in 1966 the High Court laid down that in considering whether the reason for an employee's dismissal was redundancy, and hence in determining whether he is entitled to a redundancy payment from his former employers, the industrial tribunals must consider whether the overall requirements of the employing concern for a particular kind of labour has diminished or is likely to diminish, not the addition to or subtraction of duties from a particular post; in the case which was the subject of the appeal, the High Court held that the applicant had been dismissed because he could not meet higher standards demanded, and was not therefore entitled to a redundancy payment, even though he was redundant in 'a popular sense' of the word. If the same overall amount of work is required, dismissal cannot be considered as resulting from redundancy in the meaning ascribed to that word in the 1965 Act, and the tribunal concerned had been in error in granting a redundancy payment.[2] Another example of court influence on tribunals has been the strict enforcement by the courts of the obligation laid upon tribunals by Section 12 of the Tribunals and Enquiries Act of 1958 to give the reasons for their decisions, which we shall discuss later. *Stare decisis* thus plays a sizeable role in the field of administrative justice.

[1] See p. 48 above.
[2] North Riding Garages Ltd., *v.* Butterwick, Angel, pp. 229–35.

On the other hand, desirable though adherence to precedent may seem to be in terms of consistency and predictability, it is often very hard in practice to apply precedents in the administrative field. Cases vary widely in many areas covered by tribunals, and the nature of the variation may be such as to make the application of precedent almost impossible. Flats, houses and other rented accommodation are so varied in size, condition, extent of furnishing, amenities, and so forth, that they are seldom, if ever, comparable; even where some comparison is possible, as where all the lettings considered are in the same building, the tribunal must take care not overtly to follow precedent in its decisions, for fear of falling foul of the legal doctrine enunciated in the Paddington and Marylebone Rent Tribunal case.[1] It is often impossible to compare injuries too; each will have its own effects on the subject person. A Valuation Court may find it hard to compare the smell caused by a sewage works and a tannery for the purpose of deciding how much each is worth in terms of a reduction in rateable value. Comparison becomes a useless exercise.

Sometimes tribunals evolve regular means of determining what should be done in certain circumstances; also, some tribunals are given means of determining what certain advantages or liabilities are worth, as is done in the case of medical boards and medical appeal tribunals, where various disabilities, such as blindness, or the loss of a leg, are given standard assessments.[2] Rent tribunals, with the almost unlimited discretion conferred by the duty they are given of fixing a 'fair rent', have often taken refuge in a standard arithmetical method of calculating rents, as we saw earlier.[3] The existence of such a standard system of assessment ensures at least that the decisions of any one tribunal will be to some extent consistent, and it does seem that there is a rough equity in rent tribunal decisions. In one northern city, if one took the decisions relating to single-room flats between 1960 and 1966, all described by the tribunal as 'partly furnished', the rents fixed ranged from 15s 6d to £1 17s 6d. The average rent was 19s 2d, but over half the rents fixed were between £1 and £1 10s. Also, the variation in rents could be related to the area of the city in which the properties were situated. Thus, if we take two streets, one in a fairly desirable area and the other in a poorer district, we find that in the first street

[1] See p. 9 above.
[2] See p. 78 above.   [3] See p. 31 above.

the rents fixed were one at £1 13s, and two at £1 17s 6d, while in the poorer street the rents ranged from 16s to £1 5s a week. There seems to be some correlation between the rents fixed and the amenities of the area in which the lettings are situated. As we saw earlier, however, there is no guarantee of consistency between one tribunal and another, although centrally determined methods of assessment, such as the medical board method, do ensure such consistency to some degree. One must remember that in such matters as deciding to what extent continuing disabilities resulted from industrial injury, the tribunals have an unfettered individual discretion.

The provision of a central appeal body may improve consistency, but the use of such a body tends to prolong proceedings quite considerably; one appeal against a decision to refuse sickness benefit which was taken to the National Insurance Commissioner took some eight months to hear, when it was resolved in favour of the claimant. By that time, the hardship which had resulted in the original claim was a thing of the distant past.[1] In any case, as a rule few applicants make use of further appeal provisions. Between 1959 and 1963, National Insurance local tribunals heard 211,983 cases, of which only 8,700 or 4 per cent, were appealed to the National Insurance Commissioner. Again, between 1960 and 1966, over 8,000 complaints against practitioners or chemists working in the National Health Service were heard by service committees, but only 619, or 7·5 per cent, went further. Appeal procedures are not heavily used, though they do serve to ensure a degree of uniformity, both as regards procedure and decisions.

Before leaving the subject of consistency, we might look at some statistical evidence of the degree of consistency prevailing among various types of tribunal. Taken over time, some tribunals are fairly consistent; between 1949 and 1965 the percentage of appeals against the rate of National Assistance grant in which the insurance officer's decision was confirmed ranged only from 73 to 83·5 per cent, the number in which the rate was increased varied between 16 and 24 per cent and reductions were made in between 0·04 and 0·3 per cent of the total number of cases heard.[2] Over the period, the degree of support given by the tribunals to the National Assistance Board's officers was

[1] *Shropshire Star*, 18 July 1967.
[2] Reports of the National Assistance Board, 1949–65 (H.M.S.O., 1950–66, *seriatim*).

consistent to within 5 per cent of the average. Table 1 shows that in the period from 1960 to 1966, National Insurance Local Tribunals too gave loyal and consistent support to the Department's officers:

TABLE 1

National Insurance local tribunals:
Percentage of decisions in support of insurance
officers' decisions, 1960–66

1960	74%
1961	75%
1962	76%
1963	75%
1964	74%
1965	76%
1966	75%

Again, conscientious objector tribunals in the peacetime period from 1954 to the end of conscription in 1959 show only small variations from year to year, as Table 2 shows:

TABLE 2

Decisions of conscientious objector tribunals 1954–59.[1]

Year	Unconditional registration as C.O.	Registration conditional on:		Refused
		a) doing approved civilian work	b) doing non-combatant duties with H.M. Forces	
1954	2·8	39·8	22·4	35·0
1955	2·6	40·6	17·9	38·9
1956	1·8	38·5	19·8	39·9
1957	1·2	43·0	17·2	38·6
1958	1·6	36·2	15·8	46·4
1959	2·0	39·8	14·1	44·1
Maximum Variation from Mean	±0·8	±3·4	±4·2	±5·6

[1] Information from the Reports of the Ministry of Labour, 1954–59 (H.M.S.O., 1955–60, *seriatim*).

These tribunals were not as consistent as the others mentioned, though the variations are still not large. Also, one must remember that there was no central appeal court for conscientious objectors discontented with the local tribunal's decisions; the appeal tribunals operated on a regional basis, giving more scope for variations from region to region, and from time to time, in view of the greater number of people involved in the appeal process, compared with central appeal procedures such as that provided by the National Insurance Commissioner and his deputies.

The danger that decisions may vary between one tribunal and another is always present, though it is particularly acute where there is no central appeal. Writing on the subject of Local Appeal Boards, set up under the Ministry of Labour during the Second World War to hear appeals by workmen against refusals of permission to leave employment in an undertaking scheduled as being of national import-ance, Miss D. Scott Stokes said that because there was no further appeal, the Boards' decisions varied 'chaotically',[1] while Mr Robert Pollard found that a change of chairman of a conscientious objector tribunal could make a great deal of difference to the tribunal's decisions; in one case, after a change of chairman the rate of unconditional regis-trations fell from 6 to 1 per cent of the cases heard, and outright refusals of registration rose from 9 to 51 per cent. The second chairman evidently took a far more stringent view of the extent to which patriotic duty should prevail over the demands of conscience than did his predecessor.[2]

As a result of hearing complaints of inconsistent decisions, the Franks Committee recommended that an appeal should exist in all cases, either to a superior tribunal or to the courts of law.[3] As a result of this recommendation, plus the Council on Tribunals' scrutiny of rules for new tribunals, most rules now provide for appeal on a point of law, though on questions of substance, the position is very different. From National Insurance tribunals an appeal lies to the Commissioner; medical appeal tribunals are themselves appellate bodies, yet on a point of law there is a further appeal to the Commissioner. They are, in any case, prestigious bodies, consisting of lawyers of high standing acting as chairmen, with consultants, often of professorial rank, as members.

[1] Pollard, *op. cit.*, p. 25. [2] Pollard, *op. cit.*, p. 11.
[3] Cmnd 218, paras. 105–19 and Recommendations 25–8.

G

There are fourteen of them, organised on a regional basis. In the case of agricultural land tribunals, industrial tribunals, rent tribunals, rent assessment committees and the General Commissioners of Income Tax, there is no further appeal on points of substance, and in some cases appeals from service committees of National Health Service executive councils are to the Minister of Health, not to a superior court or tribunal, an unsatisfactory position, from the point of view of the separation of judicial and executive powers. In many cases, therefore, there is still no way of ensuring equity as between one tribunal and another on questions of substance or fact, and the answer given to the question of what the parties deserve, or merit, might vary widely from one body to another, as in the case of magistrates' courts.[1]

Before considering the giving of reasons, we must remember the last of the demands made by justice on tribunal decisions; that they must conform to the requirements of the law. This is not always as obvious a truism, where tribunals are concerned, as one might suppose. The legally trained chairman often proves his worth in this respect, in that he will insist that the tribunal's decisions must be in accordance with the relevant legislation and with any precedents which are relevant and binding upon the tribunal. Sometimes, however, the demands of the law conflict with the pleas of sympathy, and it can happen that the chairman alone will insist that the law be enforced, while his lay colleagues wish to reject this course for reasons of sympathy; in one case, a National Insurance tribunal chairman found himself thus isolated; he was outvoted by his two colleagues, and as a result the Ministry appealed to the Commissioner, who upheld the chairman's views and reversed the decision. One industrial tribunal chairman saw his task as 'partly, to keep my colleagues' decisions within the bounds of the law'. Where the chairman is a lawyer, he can play this distinctive role, but, as we saw, if no member of the tribunal has a legal training it may be usurped by the clerk, who may be the employee of an interested party and in any case is not entitled to play any part in the decision-making process; he is at best an intruder, at worst, an illegitimate influence on the judges. As with the control of procedure, however, even with a lawyer chairman a certain amount still depends on the personal factor; a weak character will be a bad chairman, unable to control the words and actions of his colleagues and of persons appear-

[1] See p. 87 below.

ing before him. Other personal factors may affect decisions too; if a National Insurance tribunal chairman believes that the granting of unemployment benefit encourages idleness, very few claimants are likely to receive favourable decisions from his tribunal. Such phenomena are by no means non-existent; earlier we considered a National Insurance tribunal whose chairman shared just such an attitude with the insurance officer, an attitude shared to some extent by the employers' representative on the tribunal. As a result, very few claimants won their cases,[1] whereas at another such tribunal the chairman was far more scrupulous; he made it clear to all that he himself took an objective view of cases, and was careful to see that all parties got a fair hearing. In the second case, the chairman took pains to follow the law strictly and to explain it clearly to parties and tribunal, in contrast to the first chairman, who openly ignored the decisions of the Commissioner in one case, preferring his own moral evaluation.[2] Such variations are to a degree inevitable in a world where no two persons are alike, and on the whole the appointment of lawyers to chairs minimises the risk, since the virtues appropriate to the administration of justice are well inculcated into such persons. These difficulties are not confined to administrative tribunals, anyway. In his admirable study of the policies of magistrates' courts, Roger Hood found a similar problem; the severity of one's sentence might depend on such chance factors as the day of the week on which one's case was called; Mr Hood records that in one town included in his investigation, 'The "Monday and Tuesday Benches" . . . are made up entirely of men from the professions and business, and they are regarded as being more severe than the "Saturday Bench" of schoolmasters and trade unionists.'[3] Legal training helps to eliminate this kind of problem. Apart from this there is need for care in examining the personal qualifications of chairmen to ensure that they will be unprejudiced and that they are capable of conducting orderly proceedings. This is a duty which the centralised and heavily burdened Lord Chancellor's Department may well have difficulty in performing adequately, though the system of local recommendation of magistrates has not solved this problem either, as Mr Hood's study shows. There is a need to remember that judges, like all other administrators, are but men.

One other means of keeping a check on the entry of personal whims

[1] See p. 75 above.   [2] See p. 75 above.   [3] Hood, *op. cit.*, p. 77.

into decisions, and indeed on deviations from the requirements of law or justice, is to require adjudicatory bodies to give reasons for their decisions. Professor Richard Wasserstrom has summed up very well the case for demanding that reasons be given:

> Conceivably, at least, some judges have felt that before they render a decision in a case they must be able to justify that decision. They may have had a hunch that a particular decision would be 'right', they may have had a grudge against a particular defendant or plaintiff, but they may also have felt that considerations of this kind do not count as justifications for rendering a binding judicial decision, and that unless they could justify the decision they would give by appealing to certain other criteria, the decision ought not to be handed down as binding on the litigants.[1]

Before 1958 the practice of giving reasons was by no means uniformly adopted by administrative tribunals. Conscientious objector tribunals did not give reasons at all, although some other Ministry of Labour tribunals did. National Assistance tribunals gave no reasons either.[2] The Franks Committee made a strong recommendation that tribunals should in future be legally required to give reasons 'to the fullest practicable extent' and went on to say that written decisions were to be preferred as 'the reasons are then more likely to have been properly thought out'.[3] This recommendation was given effect in Section 12(1) of the Tribunals and Enquiries Act of 1958, which prescribes that tribunals and Ministers giving decisions after public enquiries shall give their reasons, either orally or in writing, unless they are exempted from this obligation by the Council on Tribunals, who have only granted this once, in the case of the General and Special Commissioners of Income Tax, and this not because it was felt that they should be absolved for any reason from the duty to furnish reasons, but because they were already obliged to state a case for the High Court if requested to do so, though the request must be accompanied by a payment of £1.[4] Mental health review tribunals are given a discretion to refuse to

[1] R. A. Wasserstrom, *The Judicial Decision* (O.U.P., 1961), p. 28.

[2] Information obtained from Pollard, *op. cit.*, and Dennis Hayes, *The Challenge of Conscience* (Allen & Unwin, 1949).   [3] Cmnd 218, para. 98.

[4] First Report of the Council on Tribunals (H.M.S.O., 1960), paras. 58–9. This exemption is now under review by the Council. See their Eighth Report (H.M.S.O., 1967), and p. 91 below.

give reasons to a patient if to do so would, in the opinion of medical authorities, be detrimental to his interests.[1] Otherwise, all tribunals are obliged to state reasons for their decisions if asked to do so.

Since the Act was passed Section 12(1) has been enforced with increasing stringency by the courts. The first attempt to attack a tribunal for not fulfilling its obligations under Section 12(1) concerned a conscientious objector appeal tribunal, which, when asked to give the reasons for a refusal of registration as a conscientious objector, issued the statement that 'the local tribunal decided that appellant has not established a conscientious objection to military service. The Appellate Tribunal think they were right in reaching that decision and the appeal is therefore dismissed.' So vacuous a statement of reasons could have no use so far as reassuring the applicant that justice had been given him was concerned, and he attempted to have the decision quashed in the High Court on the ground that Section 12(1) of the Tribunals and Enquiries Act had not been complied with; he failed on a preliminary point of law, and clarification had to wait upon the bringing of another case.[2]

In 1964 the position was made much clearer by Mr Justice Megaw's judgment in the case of *In Re* Poyser Mills Arbitration, involving an arbitration under the Agricultural Holdings Act of 1948, in a dispute over a landlord's request to a tenant to remedy breaches of contract, who had subsequently served a notice to quit when the latter refused to comply with the request. The Ministry of Agriculture arbitrator had endorsed the landlord's action, but the tenant then appealed to the High Court on the ground that the arbitrator had not fulfilled the requirements of Section 12(1) of the Tribunals and Enquiries Act, and won his case. Delivering judgment, Mr Justice Megaw severely criticised the arbitrator for not dealing with each of the seven issues in dispute individually, instead of which he had simply 'found as a fact that there was sufficient work required in the notice which ought to have been done and was not done on the relevant date to justify the notice to quit'. The judge went on to comment on this:

> I am bound to say . . . that a reason which is as jejune as that reason is not satisfactory . . . Parliament provided that reasons shall be

[1] Mental Health Act 1959 (7 & 8 Eliz. 2, ch. 72).
[2] *Ex Parte* Woodhouse, *The Times*, 18 June 1960, p. 12.

given, and in my view that must be read as meaning that proper, adequate reasons must be given. The reasons that are set out must be reasons which will not only be intelligible, but which deal with the substantial points which have been raised.[1]

Thus tribunals were charged to give detailed statements of reasons dealing with all the points raised in turn; the parties must be able, from the statement of reasons, to comprehend the reasoning and opinion of the tribunal on each of the points raised, and to see where and why they had succeeded or failed in their action.

In 1967, this view was confirmed in a fresh case, which also came before Mr Justice Megaw, which concerned a Minister's letter notifying a company, who had appealed against refusal of planning permission for a caravan site, of the Minister's decision to dismiss the appeal, and of the reasons for this decision. This letter, said the learned judge, was 'so obscure, and would leave in the mind of an informed reader such real and substantial doubt as to the reasons for his decision and as to the matters which he did and did not take into account . . . that, on that ground, the Minister's order must be quashed'. In the letter in question, the Minister had summarised certain parts of his inspector's report and had referred to this summary in his decision. This action was sufficient to earn the condemnation of the judge, who declared that he was 'not prepared to hold, in favour of the Minister, that the making of, and inclusion of, this summary was, or was intended to be, an innocuous and interesting and academic, but irrelevant, exercise', and since the summary made it unclear what the Minister's attitude was to other parts of the report, the order was quashed for the same reason as that given in the Poyser Mills case; not all the substantial points raised had been dealt with in the decision.[2] The courts have thus imposed a stringent duty on tribunals and Ministers. Not only must decisions be adequately clear; all points raised at the hearing must be dealt with, so guarding against judicious selections of facts to support doubtful decisions. The scope available for manœuvre has probably been narrowed as much as possible.

Indeed, the stringency of the enforcement of Section 12(1) by the courts has now caused the Council on Tribunals to think again about

[1] (1964) 2 Q.B., at 467.
[2] Givaudan & Co. Ltd., *v.* Minister of Housing and Local Government (1967), *I Weekly Law Reports*, 250.

their exemption of the General Commissioners of Income Tax from its requirements.[1] In their Report for the year 1966 the Council commented on recent developments in the courts, and remarked that the Inland Revenue tribunals might be escaping from this duty too lightly as a result of the Council's previous action. In the Report they say:

> We recommended that the decisions of these tribunals, and of these tribunals only, should be exempted because we believed that reasoned decisions would be available when requested under the case stated procedure. However, a case brought to our notice this year has caused us to doubt whether this procedure is as effective as we believed it to be in providing a means of obtaining the reasons for decisions given by the General Commissioners of Income Tax. From the papers made available to us it appeared that the reasons set out in the statement of case did not measure up to the standard laid down by recent judicial authority for reasons for decisions given by tribunals which are subject to Section 12(1) of the Act of 1958.[2] Although it was appreciated that this might have been an isolated lapse we felt it to be important to make certain that in the giving of reasons for their decisions the Revenue Tribunals were not falling below the standard required for tribunals generally.[3]

In some quarters this was regarded as tantamount to a review of the exemption of the Revenue Tribunals from Section 12(1);[4] this is to exaggerate the significance of the Council's comments, since they say in the Report that discussions with the Board of Inland Revenue were still in progress at the time of writing; nonetheless, the Council is concerned that no tribunals should escape the rigour of the standards now prescribed for them by the courts in this matter.

Nonetheless, tribunals still vary considerably as regards the giving of reasons; they can do so, since they are not required by the Act to give reasoned decisions as a matter of course; an obligation exists only if reasons are requested. Some tribunals do give detailed statements as a matter of course when they announce their decisions; such is the normal practice of industrial tribunals, for example. All the tribunals

[1] See p. 88 above.
[2] At this point the Council referred to the Poyser Mills case in a footnote.
[3] Report for 1966 (H.M.S.O., 1967), para. 69.
[4] Cf., for example, *The Guardian* for 2 November, 1967.

investigated by the present author, whether they announce their decision at the hearing or not, later send the parties to the case a written statement of the result, usually with a statement of reasons. Sometimes tribunals fear demonstrations if they announce their decision in open session; one medical appeal tribunal had had difficulties with unsuccessful appellants showering curses and abuse on their heads and had ceased to announce their decisions orally. Where oral statements are given they vary from detailed explanations of the findings of the tribunal as to facts and law, as given by the industrial tribunals and the agricultural land tribunal visited, while others confine themselves to a bare statement that having considered the facts the tribunal has reached a certain decision. This was the practice at the rent tribunals visited. Some chairmen merely announce the result, as in the case of the medical appeal tribunal which did give oral results; these were confined to the chairman saying 'Found in favour of the Minister' or of the appellant at the end of each case; it should be added that a written notification with reasons was sent out subsequently.

In their survey of rent tribunals to which we have already referred,[1] the Council on Tribunals found that in the matter of giving reasons their practice varied considerably; the statements varied 'from something almost akin to a Court Judgement to an oral explanation to the parties of the method used by the tribunal in assessing a reasonable rent, or even to a bare recital of the fact that the parties have been heard and the property inspected',[2] and the Council found that 'it seems to be the exception, rather than the rule . . . to furnish written reasons except upon request, and apparently requests are very rare.'[3] The Council's discovery of the variety of rent tribunal practice in the matter of giving reasons is valid for most types of tribunal, though the practice of industrial tribunals appears to be uniformly thorough. Because the law, though strictly enforced, only applies where reasons are requested, it has not succeeded in bringing uniform standards in the giving of decisions to the system as a whole.

Before considering public enquiries we might note that an appellant

---

[1] See p. 31 above.
[2] Report for 1961 (H.M.S.O., 1962), para. 44.
[3] 1961 Report (H.M.S.O., 1962), para. 45. A complaint about inadequate reasons given by a Rent Tribunal was made in 1967. See Council on Tribunals Report for 1967 (H.M.S.O., 1968), paras. 84–5.

body may not always regard itself as rigidly bound by its own decisions, and may develop a policy which the inferior tribunals will be expected to follow; sometimes flexibility may produce more desirable results than a strict adherence to the injunction, *stare decisis et non quieta movere*. For example, in the early postwar years, the Ministry of Labour Commissioner developed a policy that students with examinations to sit would be granted deferment of National Service for this purpose, as against earlier decisions that they should not. He decided a number of cases of this kind and subsequently both National Service officers and the National Service (Hardship) Committees whose concern such matters initially were, were ready to grant a concession which had been refused under the stress of war.[1] Administration is not entirely akin to other fields in which judicial bodies are required to function; sometimes its needs are different, and therefore the demands made on the adjudicators are different too; the analogy with the courts can mislead.

Decisions in matters which involve the holding of a public enquiry have long been a source of discontent and controversy; a discontent and controversy which first came into the open with Arlidge's case, when enquiries were firmly removed from the judicial sphere and left at the mercy of administrative discretion.[2] Since then, from time to time there have occurred outbreaks of fury over the inadequacies alleged to exist in procedures involving enquiries, and in particular, at the practice usually followed before 1958 of not publishing inspectors' reports. Lord Hewart said that public enquiries offered 'no real safeguard' to the citizen, because 'the person who has the power of deciding is in no way bound by the report or the recommendations of the person who holds the enquiry, and may entirely ignore the evidence which the enquiry brought to light'.[3] Lord Hewart urged that the inspector's report and the reasons for the Minister's decision should be published; citizens would then be able to see how much notice the Minister took of the enquiry proceedings, and, of course, it might make Ministers more chary of ignoring such reports, since they would now be seen to do so.

It must be said here that the decisions are usually taken by a group of civil servants, such as those in the Appeals Division of the Ministry

---

[1] See Pollard, *op. cit.*, pp. 21–2.   [2] See pp. 2–3 above.
[3] Lord Hewart, *op. cit.*, p. 51.

of Housing and Local Government, whose sole task is the consideration and decision of enquiry cases, and who are thus to a degree set
apart from the rest of the Department. Furthermore, the issues disputed
at public enquiries are rarely the direct concern of the Ministry whose
task it is to decide them; planning enquiries and compulsory purchase
order enquiries are usually concerned with disputes between private
citizens and local authorities; this is true of most other forms of
enquiry. As we saw earlier, the Ministry is engaged only in so far as
the local authority is seeking to give effect to ministerial policy.[1] In
the future, inspectors may be given power to decide some cases without reference to higher authority, at least in the Ministry of Housing
and Local Government, which is responsible for the holding of the
majority of enquiries, under a policy of decentralisation of decision-
making announced during 1967 by the Minister. Such delegation would
of course only occur where no issues of high policy are involved.[2]
To see the Minister as deeply involved from a partisan standpoint in
most enquiry cases would be unfair; it is an impression arising from
the fact that some other department is sometimes deeply involved, as
in the Stansted airport case, when it appears that 'the Government' is
in full array against the citizen; here the Board of Trade and to some
extent the Ministry of Technology were involved in support of the
plan. Of course, if it happens that the department holding the case is
involved, the public are rightly even more sceptical about their chances
of winning the enquiry case, but such cases are the exception rather
than the rule.

Nonetheless, following upon the Crichel Down affair, there was a
fresh outburst of discontent over enquiries. Professor H. W. R. Wade
demanded, 'Are public enquiries a farce?'[3] in 1955, and wrote that:

> The inspector usually conducts the enquiry with the greatest patience
> and fairness. But he himself makes no decision at all; he merely
> reports to the Minister. What is more, no member of the public will
> normally be allowed to see the report, so that the objectors will never

[1] For further details and an example, see pp. 38–40 above.
[2] Statement by Anthony Greenwood, P.C., M.P., Minister of Housing and Local
Government, reported in the *County Councils Gazette*, June 1967, p. 152. New
planning legislation is now before Parliament to give effect to this promise. See 1967
Report of the Council on Tribunals (H.M.S.O., 1968), paras. 22–31.
[3] *Public Administration*, 1955, pp. 389–94.

know whether their objections were effective or not. Whitehall's cap of darkness descends on the whole proceedings while the report is studied in the Ministry, and all sorts of motives and arguments may be applied to it which are beyond the ken of the objectors. Finally, after a long interval, it will be announced that the Minister has or has not confirmed the plan. Usually no reasons will be given, and there is no appeal against the final order.[1]

Professor Wade urged that 'publicity is the best policy',[2] as Lord Hewart had done a generation before.

The Franks Committee considered the question of the publication of inspectors' reports at some length, setting out in their report all the arguments on both sides, and, like the Donoughmore Committee before them, recommended publication.[3] Unlike their predecessors, their remarks were heeded, and in Circular 9/58 the Ministry of Housing and Local Government accepted this recommendation and said that reports would from henceforth be available to objectors applying within a month of the announcement of the Minister's decision.[4] The Franks Committee also recommended that Ministers should give reasons for their decisions[5] and not only was this also accepted by the Ministry of Housing in their circular 9/58, it was also enforced, as we have seen, by Section 12(1) of the Tribunals and Enquiries Act of 1958.[6] Givaudan's case directly concerned such a decision letter; reasoned decisions are now enforced on Ministers by law.

The other main bone of contention in the enquiry field has been over cases where Ministers reject their inspectors' findings. Early in the life of the Council on Tribunals it became involved in a violent controversy relating to a case in which a Minister had rejected his inspector's findings, the so-called 'Chalkpit case', which we have already discussed from the point of view of the issues it raised regarding representation; the facts are in any case well known.[7] The objectors complained, *inter alia*, that they were given no opportunity to comment on the Minister's reasons for rejecting his inspector's recommendations before the final decision was announced. The Minister had apparently based his rejection partly on information supplied to him by the Ministry of Agriculture, Fisheries and Food to the effect that the dust

---

[1] *Ibid.*, p. 390.   [2] *Ibid.*, p. 392.   [3] Cmnd 218, paras. 329–46.   [4] Para. 22.
[5] Cmnd 218, paras. 351–2, Recommendation 84.
[6] Circular 9/58 paras. 22–3.   [7] See p. 57 above.

caused by chalk mining would not adversely affect neighbouring agricultural enterprises, a major contention at the enquiry. The Council felt that the aggrieved citizens' 'feelings of injustice might well be justified',[1] and the following year they proposed new rules to govern the handling of new evidence obtained by Ministers after an enquiry had been adjourned, under which such evidence would be submitted to objectors for comment before the final decision was taken, a recommendation which was accepted by the Minister of Housing.[2] Subsequently new rules of procedure for public enquiries were drawn up by the Council incorporating these improvements and adopted.[3] Thus not only has procedure been considerably improved and tightened up, but also, when a decision is announced at the end of an enquiry, all the relevant facts are known and available for scrutiny and, where appropriate, further comment.

In view of the controversies surrounding ministerial rejection on inspectors' recommendations, and indeed, the general allegation that enquiries are merely a means whereby administrators pay lip-service to public opinion and whereby the angry can 'let off steam', it is of interest to note that the public authority's decision is by no means always upheld, and that the number of cases in which Ministers reject their inspectors' findings is small. Figures for planning appeals from 1961 to 1966 are shown in Table 3.

TABLE 3

Decisions in planning appeals, 1961–66

Year	Number of appeals heard	Number of appeals allowed	Number of cases where the Minister rejected his inspector's findings
1961	4,937	1,127	181
1962	5,361	1,350	91
1963	5,147	1,326	87
1964	5,038	1,105	181
1965	4,368	844	164
1966	4,557	844	97

[1] Report for 1960 (H.M.S.O., 1961), para. 116.
[2] 1961 Report (H.M.S.O., 1962), Appendix 'D' and paras. 58–61.
[3] 1962 Report (H.M.S.O., 1963), paras. 23–39, see p. 57 above.

Between a quarter and a third of the appeals presented are allowed each year, and only in some 3 per cent of the cases does the Minister reject his inspector's recommendations. In any case, since the Franks Committee reported, the openness of decision-making in enquiry cases has been considerably improved.

Since the 1958 Act the extent to which the organs of administrative justice must declare their reasons before the public who come to them for justice has been considerably increased, and the improvement has been secured largely through the efforts of the Council on Tribunals and the courts. Practice still varies considerably, and some tribunals are still very slack in the matter of giving reasons; the only cure for this is continuing pressure from the Council, and more persons asking for reasons so that the tribunal is obliged to discharge its statutory duty to furnish them. There are still unsatisfactory areas, notably in the field of mental health, where the tribunals have a discretion to refuse to give reasons in patients' interest; a discretion which is unchecked by any independent person or body. In the main, decisions are reasonably consistent, partly because there exists a considerable body of informal, and sometimes formal, precedent. Where precedent is informal and submerged, as it were, however, it is of no help to the citizen or his representative in deciding whether to appeal or how to conduct his case, especially since there is no body of representatives specialising in tribunal work.[1] In these cases, one of the benefits usually conferred by *stare decisis* is lost. However, in many cases circumstances are so various that precedent is but a poor guide to the tribunals; they must often decide cases on their own merits, and their duty to furnish reasons is an important check on the entry of whims, prejudices or rationalisations into the thinking of the arbitrators; rationalisation, if resorted to, must be very skilful indeed, and must in any case take all the facts of the case into account, so it probably ceases to be rationalisation. In general, the citizen can be far more certain that justice will be done than he was before 1958. Justice is more often both done and seen to be done.

---

[1] I suppose one must exclude the NCCL volunteers appearing before mental health review tribunals, but the amount of work they do is not sufficient to permit them to build up a considerable body of experience with the tribunals.

VI TRIBUNALS, ENQUIRIES AND THEIR PLACE IN THE SYSTEM

Such, then, is the system of administrative justice today. The system is still basically decentralised and sometimes chaotic, but we have seen that in a number of fields the Council on Tribunals has brought to the system both greater uniformity and higher standards, through its scrutiny of proposed rules for tribunals, through research and visits to tribunals, and through the investigation of complaints received from members of the public. Indeed, the Council has always been at pains to stress the importance of this last aspect of its work, and close links have been created between the Council and the new Parliamentary Commissioner.

With regard to the courts, always in the background are the ancient powers of prohibition, *mandamus* and *certiorari*. As a lay person, the present author would not presume to discuss the development or the working of these powers; the reader will find much on this elsewhere.[1] They are rarely used but provide an ultimate protection in cases of gross injustice. In addition, by the series of judgments which began with Corrie's case in 1918, the courts have given British administrative adjudication and decision a form distinct from that found in other countries, and distinct too from the legal system in this country, in that the overt use of precedent is severely restricted.[2] The courts have also not hesitated strictly to enforce the Tribunals and Enquiries Act of 1958 in a way which makes new demands both on authorities and upon the adjudicators; citizens are now entitled to know why it was that they won or lost their cases.

Nonetheless, there are those who say that the system is still too piecemeal; that if the citizen's rights and privileges are adequately to be protected, if he is always to be able to know where he stands in relation to law and government, there must be set up a unified system

[1] See H. W. R. Wade, *Administrative Law* (O.U.P., 1961) and J. F. Garner, *Administrative Law* (2nd edn, Butterworth, 1967) for excellent expositions of the legal position.
[2] Cf. H. W. R. Wade, 'Anglo-American administrative law: some reflections', *Law Quarterly Review*, vol. 81 (1965).

of administrative courts on the continental pattern. Despite the improvement both in standards and in uniformity of good practice brought about by the efforts of the Courts and the Council on Tribunals, the system is still varied in the extreme, as the preceding chapters have shown, and some writers have argued that this in itself is an undesirable state of affairs, and that only reform on the continental pattern can rectify this. Several academics and lawyers have written admiringly of the *Conseil d'Etat* in France, and have urged its transplanting into British administation.[1] Professor J. D. B. Mitchell, for example, has written that 'the methods of the *Conseil d'Etat* are close to those of a common law court in its use of the system of precedent. . . . It is only in such circumstances that it is at all likely that the distinct rules both of procedure and of substance which are necessary are likely to emerge.'[2]

For Professor Mitchell, only if there is a unified system of administrative courts will both administrators and the general public know what the rules are; such a system will at once give certainty to the citizen and give rise among civil servants to *une moralité administrative*; they will be careful not to expose themselves to censure in the new courts. It seems a worthy ideal, especially when one considers how frequently civil servants in this country appear to treat with disdain the rights and the feelings of the citizens they govern, but in the light of the foregoing chapters, the practicality of realising this ideal via a system of administrative courts must be called in question.

Tribunal officers are unanimous in saying that precedent is of only limited use to them, even where it can be applied at all; as one clerk put it, cases which at first appear to be similar in fact turn out to be completely different. As far as points of substance are concerned, judgments will continue to be based on the tribunal's idea of a fair settlement, with each individual tribunal to some extent evolving its own methods for deciding what is fair in their eyes. An administrative court would find itself faced with the same difficulties, and these might be increased if the court had to deal with the issues distributed among

---

[1] Cf. W. A. Robson, *Justice and Administrative Law*, the essay by J. D. B. Mitchell in D. C. Rowat, ed., *The Ombudsman: Citizen's Defender* (Allen & Unwin, 1965), M. H. Smith, 'Thoughts on a British *Conseil d'Etat*' in *Public Administration*, 1967, pp. 23–42, and C. J. Hamson, *Executive Discretion & Judicial Control* (Stevens, 1954).

[2] Mitchell, *op. cit.*, p. 278.

the many types of tribunal that exist at present; the court would find itself having to deal with a bewildering array of legal precepts and circumstances, all demanding their own standards of fairness.

The British system at least has the virtue of confining the activities of each tribunal to a limited field in which the cases bear some relation one to another; the administration of social security benefits, of redundancy payments, or of rents or rates, to cite but a few examples; if such diverse functions were combined under the jurisdiction of a single court or system of courts, the new court or courts would need to be assemblages of brilliant dilettantes. It is true that the Franks Committee urged the amalgamation of tribunals where possible, but they admitted that the practical limits to such a policy were such that few amalgamations would be possible; they advocated the greatest caution in pursuing amalgamations, since frequently the functions of the various bodies were not sufficiently cognate to permit it; the Committee concluded that they did not consider that 'there is much scope for amalgamation at present'.[1] The system should reflect in its organisation the multifarious tasks it is called upon to perform.[2]

The points at which supervision and control are vital are the interpretation of the law and the maintenance of high standards of justness; in the words of the Franks Committee, of 'openness, fairness and impartiality'. Much has been done in the first matter by the provision of further appeals on points of law, to superior tribunals or the courts. Again, there is no need for complete centralisation; most tribunals are concerned with particular statutes many of whose provisions are peculiar to themselves; no harm is done in such cases if the appeal is to a special commissioner rather than to a court, provided, of course, that the commissioner's independence is also guaranteed; in fact these officers are lawyers of the highest standing. The Council on Tribunals has done much to improve standards of procedure, even though it is a purely advisory body with no coercive powers. While most departments have been ready to give rapid effect to the Council's recommendations, there have been pockets of resistance, where the Council has met with prolonged delays in giving effect to its recommendations,

[1] Cmnd 218, paras. 135–9 and Recommendations 35, 49.
[2] The proposal for a central appellate body has been made in two forms: the General Administrative Tribunal, a piecemeal reform, and a recasting of the entire system on continental lines, but many of these objections seem to apply equally to both proposals.

or even a complete refusal; then the only weapon the Council has left is a public announcement of the department's non-cooperation, in the hope that the matter will be taken up in the House of Commons, and that public and parliamentary opinion will suffice to induce a change of heart. One other difficulty is the size of the Council's task in relation to its resources. Its maximum size is fifteen, its present budget only £20,000 a year,[1] and it has literally thousands of tribunals under its supervision.[2] As a result, it is only slowly covering the vast area of its responsibilities; for instance, it has not yet investigated the working of valuation courts. Its members only visit some nine tribunals a year.[3] The Council are aware of unsatisfactory practices in tribunals, such as valuation courts, which they have so far been unable to investigate; considerations of finance and time prevent quicker action. There is, perhaps, a case for giving the Council some 'teeth' and a larger staff, now that it is beyond the formative stage and the quality of its work has been proved. The final conclusion of our study can be that partly as a result of the Council's work, administrative justice is usually done, though perhaps it is not always seen to be done.

In relation to the other traditional guarantor of the citizen's rights and liberties, the Member of Parliament, the system finds itself in an ill-defined and somewhat uneasy relationship. If a Member of Parliament receives a complaint about a tribunal his instinct may be to attempt to resolve it himself, in order to gain political benefits which will probably accrue from success, rather than to pass it on to the Council on Tribunals. Sometimes Members of Parliament assist their constituents in presenting their cases; one Member appeared with a constituent in a test case regarding students' lodgings before a rent tribunal. Others confine themselves to informing enquiring constituents of statutory procedures to which they are entitled to have resort, perhaps assisting them to draft letters or to fill in application forms. The M.P. is another agency, like trade unions, solicitors or citizens' advice bureaux, from whom members of the public may obtain advice and assistance in their dealings with officials, tribunals and enquiries.

[1] J. F. Garner, 'The Council on Tribunals' in *Public Law*, 1965, p. 322.
[2] It does not exercise a continuous supervision over enquiries, but deals with problems and complaints as they arise.
[3] In 1967, Council members visited 22 tribunals and 2 enquiries. (1967 Report (H.M.S.O., 1968), para. 9.)

The system of tribunals and enquiries provides an inexpensive and reasonably speedy method of dispensing justice, which on the whole offers a reasonably fair chance to the citizen to put his case, and which provides for an impartial consideration of the contentions both of authority and of the individual. There is room for improvement, but under the influence of the Council on Tribunals improvements are forthcoming, if not in a flood, at least in a steady trickle. Things have improved much since the Franks Report, and today the system succeeds in being both flexible and, on the whole, just. But, as ever, the price of administrative justice is eternal vigilance.

Appendix
THE TRIBUNALS AND ENQUIRIES
STUDIED

For obvious reasons, no particular tribunal is identified here; this might result in serious embarrassment for its members and staff. A brief description of the work each type of tribunal investigated performs is provided, with reference to the relevant legislation. In all cases except rent assessment committees and agricultural land tribunals, at least two tribunals of each type listed as visited were attended, and in some cases, more than one visit was paid to a particular tribunal. Several visits were paid to each of the public enquiries listed, with the exception of the Compulsory Purchase Order enquiry, which held only one session. Since these enquiries all received considerable publicity, they are identified.

TRIBUNALS VISITED

Industrial Tribunals

Originally to deal with disputes over the obligation to pay the Industrial Training Levy (Industrial Training Act 1964); subsequently charged with settling disputes over refunds of Selective Employments Tax (Selective Employment Payments Act 1965) and with applications for Redundancy Payments under the Redundancy Payments Act 1965. Only hearings under this last statute are held in public, but they now constitute the major proportion of the work of the tribunals. Appeals on points of law only to High Court.

National Insurance Local Tribunals

To decide cases where unemployment and other National Insurance benefits have been refused by insurance officers (National Insurance Acts). Appeal to a Commissioner.

Agricultural Land Tribunals

To decide whether notices to quit served on tenant farmers should be enforced, whether a certificate of bad husbandry, also entitling a landlord to evict, should be granted, and other questions under the Agricultural Acts of 1947 and 1958, and the Agricultural Holdings Act of 1948. Also to decide

whether a landowner shall be compelled to repair a ditch causing a nuisance
to neighbours (Land Drainage Act 1961). Appeal to Courts on points of law
only.

Medical Appeal Tribunals

Chiefly to decide appeals from Medical Boards (held in private) on question
of whether a disability was the result of an industrial accident, and of the
rate of assessment of disablements (Industrial Injuries Acts). Appeal to
Commissioner on points of law only.

Rent Tribunals

To assess a fair rent for furnished lettings on application by tenants, landlords, or local authorities (Furnished Dwellings Act 1946). No appeal.

Rent Assessment Committees

To assess fair rents for unfurnished lettings in cases where the Rent Officer
has been unable to procure agreement between landlord and tenant (Rent
Act 1965). No appeal.

Valuation Court

To consider proposals by ratepayers of reductions in the gross and rateable
values of their properties; the values are originally assessed by Valuation
Officers employed by the Board of Inland Revenue (Rate Acts 1949 and
1965). Appeal to Lands Tribunal.

OTHER TRIBUNALS STUDIED (all held *in camera*)

National Assistance (Supplementary Benefit*) Tribunals

To hear appeals against decisions of officers not to make grants of National
Assistance or Supplementary Benefit,* against the rate granted or conditions
attached to grant (National Assistance Act 1949 and subsequent legislation).*

*In 1965 renamed Supplementary Benefits as a result of the merger of the
National Assistance Board with the Ministry of Pensions and National
Insurance to form the Ministry of Social Security (Ministry of Social Security
Act 1965). The tribunals are still separate from National Insurance Tribunals
(see above) but the Advisory Committees, which deal with such matters as
appointment of members, have been merged.

General and Special Commissioners of Income Tax

To hear appeals against assessments for liability to pay income tax.

N.H.S. Service Committees

Set up under Executive Councils to hear complaints against practitioners or pharmacists under contract with the National Health Service. Each committee must be representative of the professional group with which it is concerned (medical, dental, optical or pharmaceutical). Appeal to Minister of Health, or in some cases, to National Health Service Tribunal (National Health Service Act 1946 and subsequent legislation).

Mental Health Review Tribunals

To hear applications from patients compulsorily detained in mental hospitals for their release (Mental Health Act 1959).

Lands Tribunal

Appellate body for Valuation Courts, plus other functions. Highly formal, cases reported. Held in public.

Medical Boards

Tribunals of first instance in industrial injury cases. See Medical Tribunals, above.

ENQUIRIES ATTENDED

Planning Enquiry

Appeal by Messrs Capper Pass, Ltd, against refusal of planning permission by East Riding of Yorkshire County Council for chimney erection, June 1967 (Ministry of Housing and Local Government).

Compulsory Purchase Order Enquiry

Hearing of objections to proposed order of the City Corporation of Kingston-upon-Hull for the compulsory purchase of various properties in the city, May 1967 (Ministry of Housing and Local Government).

Traffic Enquiry

Discretionary enquiry into objections to proposed new waiting restrictions in the borough of Shrewsbury (Joint: Ministry of Transport and Shrewsbury Borough Corporation).

INDEX

Administrative courts
  Donoughmore Committee on, 6
  Franks Committee on, 100
  French, 4–5, 6, 12, 99
  origin of, 1
  proposals for unified system of, 6, 12,
    13, 98
Agricultural land tribunals
  and Agricultural Acts (1947, 1958),
    32
  and appeals, 86
  and arbitration, 76
  and National Farmers' Union, 69
  and precedents, 81
  decisions of, 92
  functions of, 25, 33, 34, 38, 65, 76
  members of, 66
  procedures at, 48
  representation at, 66, 68
  visited, 103–4
Air Transport Licensing Board, 30, 32,
  33
America, United States of, see United
  States of America
Angel, G., 28 n., 29 n., 30., 81 n.
Arlidge, see Local Government Board v.
  Arlidge

Barnard v. National Dock Labour
  Board, 48–9 n.
Birkett, Lord N., 60
Bradley, F. H., 79

'Chalkpit' case, 16, 57–8, 95–6
Clerks, 42–7, 51–2, 86
Commissioners of Income Tax
  and appeals, 26, 67, 86
  decisions of, 88, 91
  functions of, 26
  number of cases heard, 26

  origin of, 1
  staffing of, 43
  visited, 104
Conscientious objector tribunals
  appeals against, 85
  decisions of, 84, 88, 89
  functions of, 61
  origin of, 6–7
Corrie: The King v. London County
  Council, ex parte Corrie, 7–8, 9, 98
Council on Tribunals
  and National Council for Civil Liber-
    ties, 54–5, 70, 71
  and new rules for tribunal procedure,
    16, 42, 95–6, 98
  and Parliamentary Commissioner, 17,
    18, 98
  and procedures, 15, 17, 31, 49, 99, 100
  and public enquiries, 17, 57–8, 88,
    94–6
  and reasons for decisions, 90–1, 92, 95,
    97
  and rules for new tribunals, 85, 98
  and tribunal clerks, 42–3, 44, 45–7
  and visits to tribunals, 16, 49–50, 98
  complaints to, 16, 19, 42, 50, 57–8, 71
  establishment of, 12–13, 20
  financial resources of, 101
  functions of, 14–15, 17, 100
  influence of, 102
  problems facing, 100–1
  reports of, 15
Courts
  and reasons for decisions, 97
  and tribunals, 7, 9, 21, 48, 98
  continental administrative, 4–5, 99
  decisions of High, 3, 9, 10
  function of, 2–3
  need for administrative, 99
  system of, 1–2, 100

5